UNDERSTANDING

BASIC
HORSE CARE

YOUR **GUIDE** TO HORSE HEALTH
CARE AND MANAGEMENT

Also available from Eclipse Press

Understanding the Pony

Understanding the Foal

Understanding the Broodmare

Understanding the Stallion

Understanding Equine Business Basics

Understanding Basic Horse Care

Understanding Your Horse's Behavior

UNDERSTANDING

BASIC
HORSE CARE

YOUR **GUIDE** TO HORSE HEALTH
CARE AND MANAGEMENT

Michael A. Ball, DVM
Foreword by George H. Morris

ECLIPSE
PRESS

Essex, Connecticut

An imprint of Globe Pequot, the trade division of
The Rowman & Littlefield Publishing Group, Inc.
4501 Forbes Blvd., Ste. 200
Lanham, MD 20706
www.rowman.com

Distributed by NATIONAL BOOK NETWORK

British Library Cataloguing in Publication Information available

Library of Congress Cataloging-in-Publication Data Available

ISBN 978-1-4930-7475-4 (paper : alk. paper)

∞™ The paper used in this publication meets the minimum
requirements of American National Standard for Information
Sciences—Permanence of Paper for Printed Library Materials,
ANSI/NISO Z39.48-1992.

Contents

FOREWORD

Michael Ball worked for me here in New Jersey over 10 years ago taking care of some Grand Prix jumping horses that, at the time, I was showing both here and abroad. I remember we had good times together with the horses, and it always gives me confidence with a vet to know that he or she started in the horse business grooming, riding, and managing horses under good professional tutelage in a top stable.

Michael's new book, *Understanding Basic Horse Care*, is a must book for all of our libraries, whether we are professional trainers, teachers, riders, owners, or even curious parents. He covers it all — basic terms, soundness, disease, anatomy, grooming, etc. — in the most concise, accurate, up-to-date way possible. *Understanding Basic Horse Care* doesn't talk down to anybody; nor is it too technical for the average horse person not to want to read. It is right to the point, and Mike talks in a language we can all understand (or, at least, should learn to understand).

The big problem, as I see it today, is that while people often learn to teach, train, and/or ride quite well, they do not learn enough about the horse and his care and management. They are educated technicians in these specialties. But few of today's riders are familiar with the terms that any real horse person should know, terms relating to soundness, anatomy, grooming, and disease. In other words, they are not learning to become all-around horsemen.

Mike Ball is helping to solve this problem. Not only is he a prolific writer, adding *Understanding Basic Horse Care* to his list of literary accomplishments, he also continues to educate people through his interesting work at the College of Veterinary Medicine at Cornell University as well as helping the United States Equestrian Team on their tours of Europe.

We need to listen and learn from a man with such a profound knowledge of the horse as well as his never-ending passion. Thanks, Mike, for yet another book which I'm sure will be well-received.

George H. Morris
Pittstown, New Jersey

INTRODUCTION

I have often thought if a genie granted me one wish, I would choose to be a horse for a day. I would love to be inside a horse's head for just five minutes to see how it perceives life. Horses definitely have a language all their own, but it is possible with patience and an open mind to tap into their language.

From a health care point of view, an owner needs to know what is normal for his or her individual horse. As with people, many different personalities make up the normal horse. Some are dead calm all of the time while others need to be peeled off of the wall over any little upset.

With *Understanding Basic Horse Care*, I hope the reader will gain better insight into the maintenance and well-being of his or her horses. Knowing the normal from the abnormal is the basic foundation for good animal husbandry and veterinary medicine. An owner needs to become familiar with each horse's personality, habits, and routine behavior and more importantly, learn to recognize quickly any subtle abnormalities in a particular horse.

Because of my background and profession, much of this book has a health-oriented slant, but I also have touched upon the numerous other aspects of basic horse care. The first part of *Understanding Basic Horse Care* discusses topics of basic husbandry, such as grooming, horse housing, record keeping, feeds and feeding, stable vices, and restraint techniques, followed by a more in-depth discussion of the anatomy, physiology, and common ailments of the major body systems.

The section on basic husbandry focuses more on the day-to-day interaction an owner has with his or her horses, and the different aspects of caring and providing for a horse. This should be especially helpful for the novice owner. The anatomy and physiology section is intended to provide a better understanding of the horse as a living, breathing entity and how it interacts with its environment. For example, this section explains why respiratory diseases are so prevalent in horses, what some of those diseases and their symptoms are, and how to seek proper treatment.

In writing *Understanding Basic Horse Care*, I reflected on how the horse we know and love today evolved. I think it is important for owners to recognize this, especially in regard to how domestication has affected the equine.

The domestication of the horse has impacted its health and well-being in numerous ways. Any new task the horse has been domesticated to perform has forced it to adapt to new stresses and strains. Performance horses have adapted physically to racing, jumping, or other disciplines, but this has come with the development of specific medical problems related to the individual type of performance. For example, Thoroughbred racehorses suffer specific types of knee chip fractures related to the stresses of running on an oval track in a counterclockwise direction. More generally, domestication has impacted horses through overcrowding, lack of mobility imparted by stabling, and alterations in feeding, three factors often implicated in the development of colic. Understanding that a horse lives in an environment not of its own making can help owners appreciate why certain problems and ailments develop.

Michael A. Ball, DVM
Cornell University
Ithaca, New York

CHAPTER 1

Basic Horse Handling

Always think in terms of safety first when handling horses — safety for you, the horse, and anyone else in the general area. Like it or not, horses are fight or flight creatures and can be unpredictable when faced with new people or surroundings. With quick thinking and action, close attention to the horse's language, and some common sense, you can handle most situations safely.

A close colleague once shared a saying to help me deal with university politics: if there is going to be a battle, make sure the time, place, and person are worth it. This applies well to horses, too. For example, I was at the ring with a show hunter and needed to switch bridles. The horse went bonkers whenever the leather straps got anywhere near the ears, even bolting and running away — definitely not the time or place! So, I took the bridle apart and reattached it to the leather already behind the ears. The moral here is that there are many ways to accomplish the same task and get it done somewhat correctly. My preference is to avoid a fight with a horse if possible — it keeps the whole process more fun.

THE BARE BASICS

One of my first rules when working on a horse is to have a well-fitting halter in place and a correctly placed lead shank attached. Being prepared for the unexpected — the engine backfiring on a passing motorcycle, for instance — can prevent an accident or even tragedy.

If you want to tie up your horse, make sure it has been trained to tie. If not, don't tie the horse and expect it to stand quietly. You must be sure that the tie is solid, but will also break if a horse panicks and pulls too hard. Many of today's nylon lead shanks will not break, so use either a leather

AT A GLANCE

• Safety is the most important consideration when handling a horse.

• Always have a well-fitted halter and correctly placed lead shank.

• Lead shanks should be six to eight feet long.

• Most horses are trained to lead from the left side.

shank or rope. In addition, you can tie the end of the shank to a loop of bailing twine or a plastic wire tie, which is affixed to the actual tie. Be sure to choose sturdy objects to which to tie your horse. I remember seeing one unfortunate horse running around the show grounds, scaring the other horses, with a wheelbarrow bouncing up and down between its legs — a consequence of someone not thinking.

Lead shanks should be long enough (six to eight feet) to give you some room on the end of one if your horse acts up. My preference is a leather lead with a long brass chain on the snap end. Be careful about letting the horse acci-dentally stand on the shank

Make sure the tie can break.

while grazing or walking. Most horses will freak out when they pull back on it. If a horse pulls back with you on the end of the shank, it is generally best not to pull back in return, especially with young horses which can have a greater propensity to flip over backwards. Walk back with the horse and use voice commands to try to snap it out of whatever has triggered its flight. It sometimes takes only a little of this action to get a horse back under control. But if the horse starts to overpower you, let go. Your own safety is important. If this happens on your farm and all the horse will do is go for a gallop in the paddock, that's not so bad; but if you drop the shank at a crowded horse show, you might have to think twice about letting go.

When approaching a horse, I like to let it think that it wants to come over and see me rather than vice versa. I usually offer

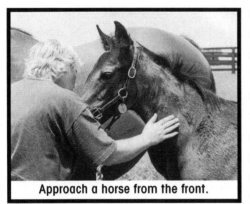

Approach a horse from the front.

my hands and let the horse come over and check me out first. After a few minutes of "making friends," I then will go about whatever I had intended to do. This can make the difference between a horse which is interested in you and what you are doing and one which wants nothing to do with you.

Horses are head-oriented animals so it is always better to approach them from the front as opposed to the rear. The domesticated horse is a left-sided animal — generally more accustomed to you working on its left side first. Since horses are creatures of habit and routine, you make the least waves by doing things the same way or as close as possible each time. Some horses don't seem to care, but most do. For example, when grooming, always start on a horse's left side and work around its butt and over to the right side. The same goes for leading a horse. Most horses are trained to be led from the left.

When turning a horse out to pasture, open the gate, lead it into the paddock, turn it around to face the gate, then let it go. Letting the horse go at the gate while it faces into the paddock is a sure way to get kicked in the head sooner or later.

Some horses do bite and like to do it. When working on a horse which bites, you usually have two choices: Stay out of range of the mouth, or if you have to be in range of the mouth, keep it on a short lead where you can maintain control over the head. For horses which kick, you have the same first choice: stay out of the way. When grooming, always let the horse know where you are and where you are going. Total hands-on contact is best. A blast from behind could occur if you suddenly grab or touch a part of

Lead from the left side.

the hind end. Many people keep kickers at arm's length, which is actually the worst possible distance. When a horse kicks, it winds up and lets fly. During the wind up, the foot is not moving very fast and has little power behind it. As the foot moves farther from the body, it gains power and speed, both detrimental to your knee caps. The place to be is close to the body, and the closer the better. You are not fast enough to get away from a kick and what usually happens is that you position yourself where the force is the greatest — behind the horse. Also, the horse's kick is straight back most of the time, so staying to the sides can be safer.

When working with a horse, two is always better than one, right? Actually the two times I have been most severely hurt by a horse was because of my helper. Rule one: If the helper is holding a horse for you while you are doing something the horse is anxious about, the helper should keep his or her mouth shut (no gossiping with other people milling about) and pay attention. Rule two: The helper always should stand on the same side as the person doing the task so he or she can see what is going on and react quickly. Rule three: The helper always should be prepared to push the horse away from you if there is a problem.

CHAPTER 2

Restraint Techniques

The first premise regarding restraint techniques for horses is knowing when and when not to use them. The individual personalities of horses sometimes make the decision to use restraint (and if so, what type) more thought-provoking than "just do it." It is often in the horse's best interest to try to determine if its reaction to whatever is being done is due to fear, stubbornness, or a bit of both. In my experience, if the animal is afraid, a more patient plan of action might work best, especially when considering the long-term outcome. If a bit of coercion can make an unpleasant task/experience more manageable, that is probably the best way to go.

But in many instances, some form of restraint is necessary. The main purpose of restraint techniques is to make an intractable horse safe to work around when attempting to do something to the horse that it doesn't like. Restraint techniques are necessary for the safety of both the people working on horses and the horses themselves. There are many times when restraint is necessary to accomplish veterinary care safely and effectively (for example, the injection of drugs or the application of eye medication). Depending on the individual horse, there are numerous other things that might require some form of restraint — ear trimming, body clipping, foot trimming, shoeing, loading on a trailer, etc. Again, for many of these tasks, the best approach might be the investment of time and a bit of coercion, but the individual horse and situation will determine this. There are numerous books which have been published by experts in the field of behavior and training that might help.

> ### AT A GLANCE
>
> • Restraint techniques sometimes are necessary for safety reasons.
>
> • Restraint devices should be applied quickly and properly.
>
> • Plan any procedure before applying a device.
>
> • There are several kinds of twitches.

The choice of restraint technique is a matter of personal preference, experience, and the individual horse. Some horses resent the initial application of certain restraint devices more than others. Obviously if World War III erupts over the application of a twitch, the whole process can be self-defeating and actually pose more danger than no restraint at all. Remember, all horses are individual and different. I have worked on several horses which go crazy if a traditional wooden handle twitch is even in sight, but a hand-held skin twitch or a hand grab on the ear are more than adequate restraint. Conversely, there are many horses which go bonkers if their ears are even looked at, but are perfectly amenable to the application of a traditional twitch. You might need to experiment with your horses to see what works the best.

APPLYING RESTRAINT

Once the decision has been made to use some form of restraint, the device should be applied quickly, properly, and with purpose. The tentative application of restraint techniques can cause more harm than good. The horse might appear to be well restrained while nothing is being done, then react with great speed when the procedure is attempted. If a restraint device is only partially applied, there is a much greater chance of the device coming off, leaving both the handlers and the horse in a potentially dangerous situation.

The procedure should be planned out and all your ducks in a row BEFORE the restraint device is applied to the horse. For example, if you need to twitch a horse to administer a prescribed injection of penicillin, have the penicillin all drawn up and ready to go prior to application of the twitch. I am not trying to insult anyone here, but I have observed many situations in which an animal is standing there with a restraint device applied (getting more wound up by the minute) while preparations for some procedure are being made which should have been done prior to the application of the restraint device. Once the restraint device has been applied the procedure should be performed as quickly as possible (without compromising whatever safety precautions are deemed necessary by the nature of the procedure being performed) and the restraint device removed. The restraint device should not be left in place any longer than absolutely necessary.

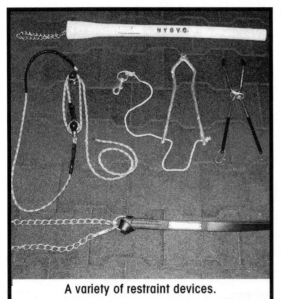

A variety of restraint devices.

Almost all of the restraint devices are applied to or around the head region of the horse. The application of restraint devices can place the handler in a dangerous position due to the proximity of the front feet. When placing any of the restraint devices on a horse, take great care to stand off to one side of the horse so if the horse strikes out or throws its head in a violent manner the handler can get out of the way more easily. Also, if there is an extra person helping (useful in twitch application), make sure that he or she is out of the line of fire as well. In addition, be careful once the restraint device is on the horse, especially if it is one of the self-attaching types. Many of these devices can become dangerous weapons should the horse freak out and start throwing its head around. This is another reason why a restraint device should be applied firmly and with purpose as the "half-applied" ones are much more likely to come off if the horse shakes its head. There is nothing more frustrating than getting hit in the head with a twitch handle while trying to work on a difficult horse.

Another tool to use with all the restraint devices is a bit of vocal intimidation. A stern, sure, and unafraid voice can capture a horse's attention and is a good start at adequate restraint. If you are doing the restraining, remember that there is a good deal of responsibility placed on you. In most cases you are restraining a horse because it does not like whatever procedure is being performed. This fact places the person doing the procedure in harm's way (kicking, biting, squashing, etc.). There also are many situations in which the horse can hurt itself or complicate certain procedures if it does not stand still or kicks out violently.

The following is obvious but needs to be said anyway. The handler has great responsibility, so this means paying attention to both the horse and whatever is being done to the horse — not eating, drinking, or gabbing. In addition, the person performing the procedure should always let the holder know when something is going to be done, e.g., stick a needle into the horse. The handler should always be on the same side of the horse as the person performing the procedure. This positioning ensures that if the horse attempts to kick, the handler can pull the horse's head in a direction that will move it away from the person in danger rather than making matters worse. Also, the horse's head should be held still. There is nothing more aggravating than attempting to look at a horse's foot or leg when it is moving its head all over the place (which shifts its weight around and kills your back). The final thing to mention here is that you must remember that if you are restraining a horse for somebody, you are taking responsibility for its safety. If you are uncomfortable with that or do not think you can do what is necessary, say so. It is better to delay a procedure than risk getting somebody hurt.

In addition to being smart about the restraint technique, be smart about your environment. Be careful not to get yourself (and your horse) boxed into an area where you can't get out of the way if the horse does explode or react violently. Also, don't restrain a horse next to a bunch of barn clutter, otherwise you might be applying a twitch to repair a laceration rather than to clip off some hair.

THE SKIN TWITCH

The skin twitch is a simple distraction that requires no special devices (except for your hand) and simply entails grabbing a large quantity of the loose skin in the neck area and squeezing as hard as you can (using a bit of a twisting action in the wrist will help with the effectiveness). To my knowledge, this technique has never been scientifically studied and could be nothing more than a simple distraction

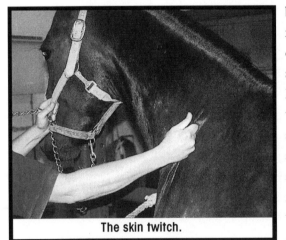

The skin twitch.

because it hurts. But it might release internal chemicals that calm the animal similar to those released with a traditional twitch. This technique is similar to scruffing a cat and is useful as a mild to moderate method of restraint in a variety of situations. An old horseman I used to work with as a groom always told me that if my "knuckles weren't turning white" I wasn't holding on tight enough. If you want to make this technique more high tech, a number of spring loaded clamps (such as those used for horse coolers or wood working) will work well if applied to the loose skin on the neck (the same holds true for restraining cats). As with all the other techniques, be careful not to get in the way of the front feet if the horse decides to strike out at you.

THE TRADITIONAL TWITCH

The traditional twitch consists of a handle (usually wood) that has a piece of chain or rope affixed to one end. The twitch is applied to the horse by standing off to one side and grabbing onto the nose with the thumb and the index finger after the rope or chain of the twitch has been placed over the fingers. The twitch then can be placed around the bundle of upper lip that has been grasped between the

fingers. During the transfer of the chain or rope, the twitch handle can be tucked under your arm so that it does not become a weapon. It helps to have an extra set of hands around to hold onto the horse's head while the twitch is being applied. After the transfer of the chain or rope, the handle of the twitch is twisted so that the chain or rope tightens on the nose. The chain or rope should be twisted up rather than down as this makes it more difficult

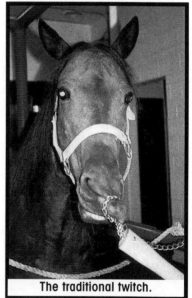

The traditional twitch.

for the twitch to come off. At this point, the twitch should be placed on rather tightly, the task completed, and the twitch removed as soon as possible. It sometimes is more effective to wiggle and alter the tightness with which the twitch is applied during the procedure as an extra attention getter. Be careful with the wiggling, because if the twitch comes off during a procedure the person performing the procedure could be placed in harm's way.

THE "HUMANE" TWITCH

The "humane" twitch now comes in a variety of styles all based on the scissor-like action of a smooth metal device. The basic premise and mechanism of action is the same as

The humane twitch.

for the traditional nose twitch, but the simplicity of this device allows for one-person application and usage. The nose is placed between the scissor-like jaws, which are closed on the nose. The device then can be "fixed" in place by a variety of mechanisms, depending on which style you have. Bear in mind that you have a metal object attached to your horse's nose now and it can be used as a weapon against you. Nevertheless, with a bit of care this device can be an extremely handy restraint tool that is easy to use and will suffice in a number of situations on a good number of horses.

THE EAR TWITCH

Grabbing on to a horse's ear is a long time method of restraint. Some people think this type of restraint is less

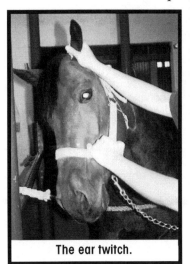

The ear twitch.

humane than many of the others, but I don't agree as long as it is done properly. I do think, right up front, that the application of any type of mechanical twitch to the ear is inappropriate and should not be done. The cartilage in the ear is very sensitive and can be permanently damaged if the ear is handled too roughly. On the other hand grabbing onto the ear and squeezing with a mild turning action can be an extremely effective, as well as a quick and easy technique for short-term restraint in a variety of situations. Some horses are extremely submissive to the ear twitch whereas others can react with sudden and strong resentment. Most horses which resent the grabbing of their ear become submissive if you don't let go during the initial resentment. There are some horses which just don't go for this and another method of restraint must be chosen. Again, think of your safety while applying an ear twitch technique and stay out of reach of striking feet or head butts.

THE CHAIN SHANK

The chain shank can be a trusty lifesaver and should be present on every horse farm. When shopping for a good lead shank with a chain on the end, pay great attention to the length of the chain. It must be long enough to be passed through the side rings on the halter and connect back to itself. The shank should be passed through the left ring on the nose piece of the halter, over the nose in direct contact with the skin, through the right ring on the nose piece of the halter and then either of two things: 1) passed through the ring under the noseband and attached back to itself or 2) passed up to the halter ring near the eye on the right side (my preference is the former). These are probably the main two of a variety of methods for attaching a chain lead shank to a horse. The one way I think is wrong is to just pass the shank from the nose ring on

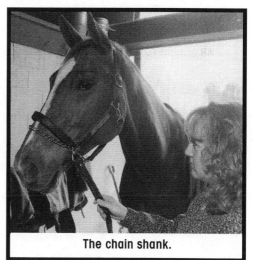

The chain shank.

the left side to the nose ring on the right side and stop — the one thing this technique accomplishes every time is to pull the halter into the right eye every time the shank is pulled!

The chain shank, when used in this manner, is an attention getter, but can be ignored by many horses if they are wound up enough.

If just having the chain over the nose is not enough to get their attention, the chain can be slipped down their nose and under their upper lip onto the upper gum surface or in their mouth. This method of restraint can be profound, but must be used carefully — it is generally not necessary to be very rough when using this technique. If I choose this technique, my preference is to place the chain under the upper lip. I am not much of a fan of the chain in the mouth. If used with respect this technique is humane and useful in a variety of restraint situations. Again, be careful not to get in the line of fire when placing the chain under the horse's lip.

THE "STABILIZER"

A recently marketed product called "the stabilizer" makes use of the restraint principles offered by the old "war bridle." The device is made of rope similar to that used for rock climbing with some special additions, including a block and

The stabilizer.

tackle type pulley system. The device is placed on the horse's head so that the pressure points at the poll and under the upper lip are affected. Once the device is in position, the rope is tightened using the pulleys and can be fixed in place allowing for one person usage. The mechanism of action is reported to be the same as with other twitches and to release brain chemicals in much the same way. There is an association between the pressure points affected by the stabilizer and known acupuncture points. I have found this manner of restraint to be extremely easy to use and effective in a variety of situations on a variety of horses. This method of restraint is very humane and extremely effective at the same time. It is rapidly becoming one of my favorite methods of restraint for difficult horses.

CHEMICAL RESTRAINT

Many times the use of sedative drugs can help greatly in accomplishing tasks that horses don't like. There are a variety of drugs currently available for sedation that can be prescribed by your veterinarian. This method can be very useful for young horses and make their first experiences with unpleasant procedures less unsettling. The sedative drugs can have negative side effects and should be used only under a veterinarian's supervision. In addition, remember that the American Horse Shows Association does not consider hair clipping or shipping a "therapeutic" use of the sedative drugs. If using sedatives for these sorts of procedures, be sure to

A sedative can be helpful.

find out the minimum withdrawal time for the specific drug used before competition. If you have a horse which is extremely difficult about certain situations, sedation might be the easiest on everybody (including the horse).

CHAPTER 3

Housing the Horse

If you are in a position to have a facility constructed from scratch, do as much research as possible before spending any money. Tour many other facilities and see what works and what doesn't. The important considerations are space, drainage, and ventilation. From a space standpoint, a general rule of thumb is a minimum of two acres of pasture per horse. Even with that guideline followed it is difficult to maintain a pasture, which is a science unto itself. Substantial information exists that can help you with the concept of pasture rotation, re-seeding, fertilizing, treating, and cleaning.

For horses which live outside year round, you will need to build at least one shelter. The shelter will guard against the sun, rain, snow, and wind, and needs to be strategically placed based on such consid-erations as the direc-

A run-in shed provides shelter.

tion of the prevailing wind and the location of high ground. You will always need to address the water source and how to keep it from freezing in the winter (if this is a concern in your area). Also, don't forget that outside waterers need to be cleaned regularly. In addition, any electrical connections for water heaters can require significant maintenance.

Barns come in all shapes and sizes and in many different materials. If building, learn as much as you can before deciding on a barn.

AT A GLANCE

- Two acres per horse is the general rule.

- Horses living outside need some kind of shelter.

- Ventilation is an important consideration for stabled horses.

- Some horses develop stable vices, such as cribbing or wood chewing.

For horses which spend all or some of the time in a barn, I prefer 12 x 12 box stalls. Ventilation is extremely important and should be incorporated into the design and construction of a barn. Many respiratory diseases can be linked to poor ventilation. Also, guard against creating poor ventilation. In our ever-present need to domesticate the horse, humans tend to think that if we need one thing or another, horses must need it, too. Many barns are sealed up tight as can be in the winter to keep the horses warm. Horses don't need to be kept nearly as warm in the winter time as we think. Good ventilation is more important. I prefer to crack the windows and blanket the horses if they are cold and need extra warmth. If horses are allowed to grow their winter coats

A roomy, well-ventilated stall.

The downward slope from the stalls can help with drainage.

and eat plenty of hay (remember the digestion of hay provides more body heat than that of grain), they really don't even need blankets. If they are show horses with full body clips in the dead of winter, that's a different story and extra blankets generally are required.

From a drainage standpoint, make sure both the pastures and barns are not on a flood plain. Excessive dampness can cause a variety of health problems and make general care of the facility more difficult. For the stalls, plan on some type of drainage system for urine. If the stalls have poor drainage, then more frequent cleaning is important. It also is important to use enough of an absorptive bedding to allow for adequate cleaning and comfort. The ammonia fumes that can be created by urine in the bedding can predispose to respiratory disease.

STABLE VICES

A stable vice is an undesirable behavior demonstrated by horses which are stall bound but also in pastures or small paddocks. The most common stable vice is probably "wind sucking," commonly known as "cribbing," followed by wood chewing, stall weaving or walking, and fence line pacing. The stable vices are classified as "compulsive" behaviors and termed by some as true addictions. There is scientific evidence that the compulsive vices cause a release of endorphins, chemicals in the brain that act like opiate narcotics, such as morphine. The endorphins cause a general feeling of well-being, which long-distance runners often note when they reach a point where these chemicals are released by the body. It has been demonstrated that drugs which block or reverse the effects of the endorphins will halt the stable vice temporarily. Researchers do not know what factors lead to the development of cribbing, but it is often attributed to some degree of boredom.

Cribbing is the act of sucking air into the throat. The horse usually rests its teeth on an object such as a board, feed manger, or bucket, and arches and contracts the neck muscles while letting out a belching type of sound as the air is gulped. Cribbing raises several concerns. Some people think that a cribbing horse might "teach" the vice to other horses in the barn. To my knowledge, no research supports this and there is rarely a barn full of cribbing horses. Another concern is that cribbing can lead to colic, although no scientific evidence suggests that cribbers are predisposed to health problems. The chronic cribber can cause a good deal of damage to its incisor teeth and destroy stall doors, feed mangers, buckets, and almost everything else it attacks in the effort to crib. Some horses are so obsessive about cribbing they will attempt to do it on people if given the chance.

Cribbing is a compulsive behavior.

The desire to intervene and try to end cribbing varies with individual owners, and the success varies with individual horses. There are a number of commercial devices available, such as cribbing straps or collars that have a variable degree of success. The first thing to do is remove all objects on which a horse might crib, but for the extremely obsessive horse even a crack in the wood or a small nail head will do. In addition to these interventions, there are several surgical procedures which have evolved as a potential treatment. In these procedures several of the long muscles on the neck are cut in an effort to prevent the neck arching necessary for cribbing. In addition, one of the surgical procedures cuts the nerve that connects to muscles necessary for neck movements. If your horse is a cribber and you worry about health implications, consult with your veterinarian about potential treatment options.

Another stable vice that can be extremely destructive is

Wood chewing can be destructive.

wood chewing. For the vigorous wood chewer it is only a small task to create portholes all over the stall as well as destroy paddock fences. There are numerous commercial products available to spray or paint on the wood to prevent chewing. Again, the success of these products depends on the obsessiveness of your horse. I have had a horse immediately start gnawing on wood just sprayed with fresh Tabasco sauce without missing a lick.

Stall weaving or walking is another common vice often attributed to confinement, boredom, and/or lack of social interaction with other horses. As with all the other stable vices, making an attempt to relieve boredom can help. Feeding a greater amount of roughage/hay (generally a good thing anyway) and a reduced amount of concentrate/grain also can help. In addition, a greater amount of turn-out with companion horses might offer increased social interaction and thereby reduce the compulsive behavior. For some horses, the introduction of a companion/buddy such as a pony can help. In addition, goats can make good companions for some horses. In cases where some of these common remedies fail, consult with your veterinarian and/or an animal behavior specialist to determine a potential solution to the problem.

CHAPTER 4

Feeding and Preventive Medicine

The topic of feeding will be touched on only briefly due to the enormous number of existing books and information on the subject. One of the main points to remember is that any changes in feed routine must be made slowly in an effort to reduce the chance of colic. If you are in a situation that requires changing feed, try to mix the old with the new to allow a transition. Also, if you go to shows it is always a good idea to bring some of your own feed products along.

There is a large body of research developing that implicates high-energy, high-protein diets in the occurrence of developmental bone disease in young, rapidly growing horses. There are many sources of guidelines for feeding growing horses. In addition, the higher carbohydrate diets (high grain diets) have been associated with certain muscle problems in performance horses.

Horses naturally are foragers.

The horse's digestive system acts like a fermenter. Much of the many feet of equine intestine acts as a fermentation chamber. The gastrointestinal tract is populated by a large number of bacteria that have the ability to break down the fiber (hay/grass) and produce products that are absorbed from the gut and used for energy. Anything that can disrupt this delicate fermentation has the potential to play havoc with the intestines. Although grain products might be necessary to make up for the loss of nutrient value in the grasses (the process of making hay decreases the nutrient value of the grass), remember that the horse's intestine evolved to handle fiber, not grain products.

I think most of the medical problems related to the gastrointestinal system result from overdomestication of the horse with respect to feeding. The horse is a grazing animal which evolved to eat fiber with a high water content (grass) continuously for about 18 hours a day. We have changed that to feeding a low water content fiber (hay) in larger quantities eaten in a shorter period of time. That, in combination with a greatly reduced amount of exercise (the average horse is relatively stall bound) and the addition of more rapidly digested/fermented grain products, has the potential to "overwhelm" the gastrointestinal system. These are difficult issues to contend with due to the way many of us have to manage horses given geography, economics, etc., but I do think this all relates to colic. Pasture is important for both nutrition and exercise. I think no expense or effort should be spared on tracking down and buying the best quality hay that can be found and shipped in — it is a much more important investment than grain.

Another misconception is the increased feeding of grain products in the colder months to provide extra calories for "heat." A great deal of the horse's normal "body heat" comes from the fermentation of fiber within the gastrointestinal

> **AT A GLANCE**
>
> • Changes in feed should occur gradually.
>
> • Fiber such as grass and hay should form the bulk of a horse's diet.
>
> • The average horse needs about 3% of its body weight in fiber per day.
>
> • The most important vaccine is tetanus.

system. It has been demonstrated that the digestion of hay actually produces a significantly higher amount of heat than any

Feed more hay in winter months.

of the grain products. So, if you are trying to keep your horse warm in the winter months, don't feed less hay and more grain — just feed more hay.

What do you feed a new horse? Like people, horses are all different, but there are some simple rules of thumb. I think all horses should be weighed and fed according to their weight, with feed adjusted based on subsequent changes in weight. If a scale is not available, the use of weight tapes is actually fairly accurate and is better than just guessing. The rule of thumb for the average, adult horse, in an average amount of work is to feed 3% of its body weight in fiber per day. This also requires having the ability to weigh the feed (both the hay and the grain — not just a coffee can worth). So, the 1,000-pound horse can be started with 30 pounds (3% of 1,000 pounds) of hay per day split up into three or four feedings.

If you feed some grain, the next rule of thumb is that 10% of the amount of fiber, three pounds in this example, can replace that part of the fiber — so this horse can start at 27 pounds of hay and three pounds of grain per day. This obviously will vary with the individual horse and the individual quality (nutrient content) of the hay and grain. To get even more high tech, the hay and grain can be analyzed (see your veterinarian or a feed consultant) for energy content and the ration specifically calculated based on the analysis. In addition, there are more detailed nutritional requirements published by the National Research Counsel which take into consideration such specifics as age, work load, etc. The average, middle-aged horse in light work has a daily energy requirement of approximately 18,000 calories.

PREVENTIVE MEDICINE

Vaccination and deworming programs vary greatly and depend on such factors as geography, the number of horses on a farm, whether a horse travels, and whether it is a brood animal. It is best to consult with your veterinarian to form

preventive vaccination and deworming programs that are right for your set up. The most important vaccine is tetanus because all horses can get and do die from tetanus. Failing to vaccinate your horse for tetanus is negligent. Other vaccinations typi-

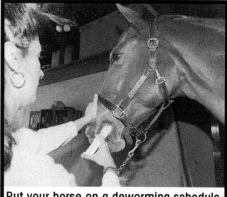

Put your horse on a deworming schedule.

cally include eastern and western equine encephalomyelitis, equine influenza, equine rhinopneumonitis (Herpesvirus), Potomac horse fever, strangles (*Strep. equi*), and rabies.

Deworming typically is performed four times per year, but might be necessary more or less frequently depending on your individual situation. There also is a daily deworming product available that might be right for some situations. In addition, I think it is a good idea to have a complete veterinary examination once a year which would include checking the teeth and performing any dental work necessary at that time.

The best preventive medicine is for you to become familiar with your individual horses and learn how to perform a basic physical examination. You should be able to obtain their heart rate, respiratory rate, and body temperature. There are many excellent references that can help you learn more about basic veterinary care and first aid.

CHAPTER 5

Grooming

Doing a thorough grooming before and after every ride will help keep your horse shiny and healthy looking as well as potentially alerting you to any brewing health problems.

I usually start on the left side of the horse when beginning to groom. I begin by currying the shoulder, neck, back, stomach, rump, and upper part of the legs (the bottom of the legs is too sensitive to use a curry). I then use a stiff brush to get the heavy dirt off first, working my way over the body, down the legs, over the mane, top part of the tail, and lightly over the face unless the horse objects. Next, I repeat the procedure with a soft brush, paying a lot of attention to the face.

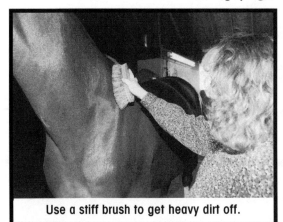

Use a stiff brush to get heavy dirt off.

I repeat with a towel or soft cloth, wiping the eyes, nose, and mouth after going over the entire body.

I like to use a comb — plastic is preferred — on the mane and forelock. I then comb the tail carefully, starting at the top and holding my hand around the base, moving downward. Doing this as little as possible is best as the tail is quite fragile and will break off easily. Finish up by using a damp-to-wet brush to brush the mane, first over the left side, then the right. For manes that don't lie down, combing as you wet it helps a great deal. Also, check the ears as you go and unless the horse objects, wipe them inside with a towel or damp sponge.

The hooves are very important because horses spend the majority of their life on their feet and you have to help in any way you can. I like to listen to what the farrier has to say about their condition and any recommendations he or she might have. A commercial hoof packing will work well on dry feet for a couple of days at a time, especially if the horse is being ridden on a hard or very rocky surface. Applying hoof packing in the stall works best. Fitting a piece of paper over the hoof to keep the packing in place is a good idea. Also, keep an eye on any stud holes in the shoe. If you show a lot, they are usually easy to maintain, with the constant putting in and taking out. I like to use either the pre-cut, oiled cotton wads you can buy in tack stores or you can make your own with the soft cotton ball-type cotton. The older the shoes get, the more likely that the stud holes become stripped, so you want to check them before going to a show or event.

As for the sole of the foot, I like to apply some hot Venice of Turpentine a couple of times a week on just the sole, not the frog — it gives it a tough layer that helps keep the hoof strong. Ask your farrier if you have any questions.

BATHING

A whole book could be written on bathing. I prefer to bathe a horse as little as possible, but some people think it's a way of grooming and give baths frequently. If you live in a hot, dusty climate you're apt to have to bathe a lot, but try not to if the horse is being ridden at home and doesn't get hot and sweaty. Brush instead.

Frequent bathing tends to dry the skin and unless you have time to dry the head, legs, and stomach well and to make sure the horse is warm enough afterward, try to avoid the bathing routine and opt for a thorough grooming.

For bathing a dirty horse, I like to use a commercial horse shampoo that is mixed with water. Scrub with a sponge, paying attention to the mane and tail. You might have to use a small handful of soap to scrub the mane and tail manually as well as the lower legs if they are particularly muddy. I like to do the whole body, then tackle the head, making sure not to over soap or get shampoo in the horse's eyes or ears. I also like to use my bare hands to scrub around the eyes and ears and forelock after squeezing a soapy sponge over the face gently.

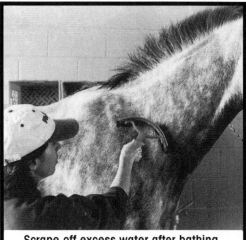

Scrape off excess water after bathing.

Then you should scrape the body with a plastic, metal, or whatever scraper you like, starting at the top of the neck and working your way down. Go over the stomach and upper parts of the legs repeatedly until no water is dripping. Use a dry sponge or your bare hands to run down over the lower legs, front and back. Then towel dry the face first, followed by the legs and belly. Taking the time to rub a horse dry with a towel will reward you with a lovely shine. Also comb the mane while wet (not the tail) and if you like, spray a product such as Show Sheen™ or something similar in the tail, but not on the body.

For cooling out a hot horse, a swig of Vetrolin™ in the water is great but otherwise plain water is fine. Repeat the same techniques for soap bathing for a cool-down bath. If the weather is brisk or cold, put a cooler or mesh cover over the horse until it is dry. After a good bath simply brushing the horse with a clean, soft brush is all that is needed as well as taking care of the mane, tail, and feet.

Gray horses really don't need care that's too much different, except occasionally or before a show or event. Use a whitening shampoo and follow the directions on the bottle. A clean halter, blanket, and cooler will keep your horse whiter longer.

CLIPPING AND BRAIDING

Pull or trim the mane to keep it at a length to your liking, using either a metal pulling comb if the mane is long and thick or scissors if the horse objects too much. Some people are adept at the scissor look. One of my preferences for almost any horse is to use a clipper blade (preferably a No. 10 blade or a body clipping blade). You trim from underneath and after some practice (not before a show) it looks great. Using this technique on a thin mane will eventually return some body and thickness to the mane so that some actual pulling will make it neat and trim.

Braiding the mane over with elastics is good for training the mane to lie down on the correct side; doing this after the mane has been washed helps the most. If you prefer, making small pony-tails of the first half of the mane (from the skin to the middle) with the elastic is quick and easy and

Trimming the ears with clippers.

also will help train the mane. Braiding for the show ring should be done with yarn. Try to learn from a professional, who can show you the right tools and techniques.

Trimming the horse's ears, legs, and whiskers is done for

show horses so they look neat and tidy. Some people like to keep this look at home as well. I like to trim the whiskers with small clippers designed for the face and lower legs. The variety of blades varies from No. 30 to No. 40, which cut very close for whiskers. Some also like this cut for the inside of the ears. The next blade up is a No. 10 or No. 15, generally used for clipping the long hair between the jawbones and on the lower leg, whether completely from the knee down or just the fetlock and coronary bands. I prefer a disposable razor for the muzzle. After dampening the nose area and going gently over the whiskers, a nice close shave is obtained and most horses seem to enjoy the feeling. I like to trim before going to a show, sometimes a day or two ahead of time.

If you have to use a twitch, make sure it is the "humane" type twitch. Always try to have someone help you as some horses object to any twitch. The wooden handle twitch is good when you have a helper and you should always stand to the side of the horse because some will try to strike with the front feet or plow you over. Never keep a twitch on for very long as it makes the horse angry and their lips become numb. Another useful tool now available is the "stabilizer," which works on poll pressure and under the upper lip. This can be a calming device used at the same time you trim or perform other tasks or procedures.

As for body clipping, you shouldn't attempt this for the first time alone. Horses react in some dangerous ways to the noise, sound, and feel of the large clippers. I like to let the horse grow a good full coat in the fall/early winter if possible. If your horse is getting hot, sweaty, and won't dry well, clipping will help keep him healthier and your life easier. The full body clip is a must for horses going to a lot of the big indoor shows, but I find clipping just the body and head with the big clippers and leaving the legs from the elbow down and from the stifle down keeps the horse warmer. Also, the trace clip is good for those who want a horse to cool out more quickly, but they don't need blankets afterwards.

As for clipping the entire head, I prefer the larger body clippers unless you are well experienced with the small clippers, which clip much more closely and give a very different look. After clipping the body, you'll need a sheet or a sheet and blanket as the temperature drops. You have to test your horse's body temperature after he has been clipped. Put some clothes on him if the rump, shoulder, and/or ears feel cold. If turning out a clipped horse, invest in a turn-out blanket (rug). If it is very cold and your turn-out rug fits well over your sheet and/or blanket you can leave them all on. You should test how they will stay in place by having your horse wear it to bed one night — it will show you if it will work outside without becoming too much of a mess.

THE LEGS

Learning about your horse's legs is extremely important. Run your hand down them daily as part of your grooming routine or just feel them as you feed in the morning and evening. You will learn when there is any heat, swelling, bumps, sensitivity, cuts, scrapes, and all sorts of things you can catch before they become problems.

I like to leave the legs un-bandaged as much as possible, so that when you have a problem you can bandage and do some real good. All horses should learn to wear wraps at one time or another so you won't have

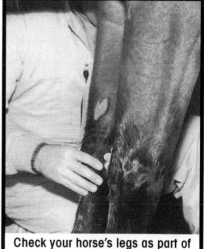

Check your horse's legs as part of the daily grooming routine.

to worry about them getting used to it when the time comes. Bandaging for shipping is a must unless you have a horse which has no shoes or you know will kick the hind wraps down. Try them overnight in the stall if there are any questions about whether the horse will stand having them on.

I also like to bandage after any really hard work or lots of jumping, using plain alcohol or witch hazel full strength rubbed in lightly or any of the stronger liniments for strains or sprains. If you suspect any significant injury, you should always consult with your veterinarian.

Use caution with poultices. They are great when used overnight, but can backfire and cause bigger problems with any deep cuts or even smaller abrasion. You should never poultice over an open wound or any wound you suspect is infected. Using poultices on a daily basis is not useful unless the horse is jumping hard and has some problems.

Begin by using a ready-made poultice. Have the poultice, a bucket of water, and some rolled paper. Don't use paper with colored ink on white legs! Take the rolled paper and soak it in the water. Next, have your bandages ready to use with all this within reach. First, dampen the legs with your hand or a sponge. Next, spread the poultice up and down the leg as thinly or thickly as the directions call for; it generally goes thickest on the tendons. Avoid putting it on cuts or don't poultice at all if you are unsure. You also can put some gauze squares directly over a small cut and avoid getting poultice on that area. Next, squeeze the excess water out of the paper and put it around the leg, using some leftover poultice from your hands to seal it to itself. Then put your cotton bandage on as usual. Don't have the poultice below the ankle unless otherwise needed. If you are poulticing low, then the bandage should be longer.

As far as poultice removal, some are easier to remove if you let them dry and brush them off or if you use the paper as a way to wipe most or all of it off. You can put on some kinds of poultice above the hocks and knees and you don't have to bandage these parts. I try to wash the legs only when really dirty or when any cuts are present. Drying the legs after washing is very important in avoiding problems related to wet heels/pasterns such as scurf and the development of scratches.

(Martha Bowen, a professional groom who has cared for horses competing on the U.S. Equestrian Team, including two Olympics, contributed to this chapter.)

CHAPTER 6

Conformation and Locomotion

My goal in discussing conformation is to point out some of the basic thoughts on the topic and to describe many of the well-known conformational faults. The "construction" of the individual horse imparts on it the ability to perform in a mechanically correct manner. "Conformation" describes this construction and proportionality of body parts. The word "type" describes those things of personal preference, but certain conformational correctness is common to all types.

Conformation is defined as the "form" or "outline" of an animal and often is discussed in terms of form and function. It is important to recognize conformational faults of the limbs as they often contribute to if not actually cause lameness. Conformation is inherited and therefore should be taken into consideration with breeding animals. There is no perfect formula for success when breeding for a "correct" individual. This mainly applies to performance horses because poor conformation is less likely to matter with the backyard pleasure horse (both of my horses fall into the latter category and often are used as teaching examples for poor conformation at the university). However, there are plenty of poor performers with great conformation and vice versa. There are many factors that enter into the making of a great performance horse.

On the subject of general conformation, I usually follow the writings in the classic veterinary textbook: Adams' *Lameness in Horses*, recently revised by Ted Stashak of Colorado State University. The first edition of this splendid bible of lameness (the book is now in the fourth edition) appeared in 1962. As described in Adam's text, the common denominator in conformation is balance. A horse with perfect conformation is a horse which is exquisitely balanced. To appraise balance,

AT A GLANCE

• Conformation is the arrangement of a horse's body parts.

• Faults in conformation can contribute to or sometimes cause unsoundness.

• Locomotion dictates the way a horse moves.

• A horse has four basic gaits — the walk, trot, canter, and gallop.

divide the horse's body into three equal parts by visually drawing a vertical line from the level of the point of the elbow to the top of the withers and from the point of the hip to the front aspect of the stifle. These imaginary lines should assume a perpendicular relationship to the ground surface and roughly divide the body into head, neck, and forelimbs; body; and hindlimbs. In addition, a line drawn from the point of the shoulder to the center of the stifle should be parallel to the ground surface.

The head and neck are used in balancing the body, so a long and slender neck with a balanced proportional head is desireable. The horse's center of gravity is located near the center of the rib cage, placing it forward on the body. This means the forelimbs bear approximately 65% of the body weight. Due to the forward location of the center of gravity, it takes only slightly more height at the croup compared to the front end to shift a significant proportion of weight onto the forelimbs.

Limb conformation is very important and in general the legs should be well suited to body height, depth, and length. The limbs should be straight and bear weight equally. The toes should be pointed straight forward and the feet should be as far apart on the ground as the limbs are where they attach to the chest or the hindquarters. The chest should not be too narrow, and a plumb line dropped from the point of the shoulder should cut the limb equally in half throughout its length. When viewed from the side, the forelimb should be straight to the fetlock and the fetlock should slope forward to the ground through the foot in an even, unbroken angle. The hindlimb should do the same from the hock down. The cannon bone should be perpendicular to the ground.

Looking at a lot of horses can help you become a better judge of conformation. A good place to learn is at horse shows where conformation classes can be observed or by looking at horses selling at auction. These sources can help you learn what "type" is important to various breeds as well as conformation basics.

The following is a list of common conformation faults considered undesirable in the horse:

Base narrow — The distance between the center lines of the feet at their placement on the ground is less than the distance between the center lines of the limbs at their origin in the chest.

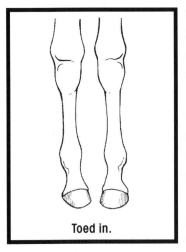

Toed in.

Base wide — The distance between the center lines of the feet on the ground is greater than the distance between the center lines of the limbs at their origin in the chest.

Toed in or Pigeon-toed — The toes point toward one another when viewed from the front.

Toed out or Splay-footed — When viewed from the front, the toes point away from one another.

Calf knees or sheep knees — Posterior deviation of the carpal joint, a weak conformation, and the legs seldom remain sound.

Bucked knees or knee sprung (goat knees, over in the knees) — A frontward deviation of the carpus. It generally causes less trouble than the calf knee condition.

Knock knees or knee narrow — Medial (inward) deviation of the carpal joint toward each other.

Bow legs or bandy-legged — Outward deviation of the carpal joint when viewed from the front of the horse.

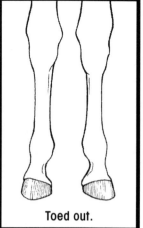

Toed out.

Open knees — An irregular profile of the carpal joint when viewed from the side.

Offset knees or bench knees — The cannon bone is offset to the lateral (outer) side and does not follow a straight line from the radius. Predisposes to medial (inside) splints.

Tied-in knees —- Viewed from the side, the flexor tendons appear to be too close to the cannon bone just below the carpus. Viewed from the side, this condition causes a "cut out" appearance just below the carpus on the anterior (front) surface of the cannon bone.

Standing under in front — A deviation in which the entire forelimb from the elbow down is placed back of the perpendicular and too far under the body when the animal is viewed from the side.

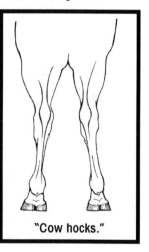

"Cow hocks."

Camped in front — The entire forelimb, from the body to the ground, is too far forward when viewed from the side.

Cow hocks — Medial deviation of the hock. The limbs are base narrow to the hock, and base wide from the hock to the feet.

Sickle hocks — Excessive angulation of the hock joints.

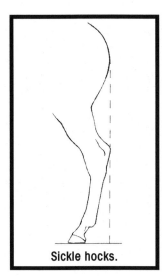

Sickle hocks.

When viewed from the side, the angle of the hock joint is decreased so that the horse is standing under from the hock down.

Straight behind — Excessively straight legs. When viewed from the side there is very little angle between the tibia and femur, and the hock joint is correspondingly straight.

Flat feet — A flat foot lacks the natural concavity in the sole. It is not a normal condition in light horses, but is present in some draft breeds.

Dropped sole or "pumiced foot" — The sole has dropped to, or beyond, the level of the bearing surface of the hoof wall.

Brittle feet — Usually associated with dryness of the atmosphere and lack of moisture in the soil, and are more apt to occur in unpigmented or white feet.

Buttress foot — A bone growth on the extensor process of the third phalanx or coffin bone (from low ringbone or a fracture). Swelling on the front surface of the hoof wall at the coronary band results. A squaring of the toe from the coronary band to the ground surface, a result of deformed hoof growth, is caused by chronic inflammation.

Club foot — The foot axis is 60° or more. Probably related to deep digital flexor tendon contracture in young horses.

Coon-footed — The pastern of the coon-footed horse slopes more than does the anterior surface of the hoof wall. In other words, the foot and pastern axis is broken at the coronary band.

LOCOMOTION

Locomotion is at the very heart of what most domesticated horses do for a living. The way a horse moves (specifically) often is taken for granted. Locomotion is directly linked to conformation as it dictates "the way a horse moves." Again, there are differences depending on the type. For example, the Morgan horse will have a different nature to a particular gait than a Thoroughbred. The Morgan will have higher "action" (raise its legs higher) than the Thoroughbred, but the basic principles of locomotion will be the same.

The horse's legs should move in a straight line when watched from behind — the leg should track straight and be perpendicular to the ground. The foot should hit the ground evenly and in a slight heel-to-toe manner. When viewed from the side, the length of stride should be equal from side to side and all of the angles of flexion (the fetlocks, carpus, hocks, etc.) equal when compared from side to side. If the stride length is shorter on one side or the degree of movement of a particular joint is different, this could signal a lameness problem. Stride length is typically shortened on the lame leg. In addition, changes in stride length or joint movement trigger changes in weight distribution and balance throughout the body. For example, when a lame foreleg becomes weight-bearing, the horse usually moves its head and neck upward and slightly away from the lame leg. These movements further shift weight off of the painful limb. A similar movement occurs in the pelvis in a hind leg lameness.

It is important to understand the basic gaits. The four basic gaits are the walk, trot, canter, and gallop. The walk is what is known as a "four-beat gait" and two feet always maintain contact with the ground. The gait is from side to side as both feet on one side of the horse (e.g., right front and right hind) hit the ground before the two feet on the opposite do. The

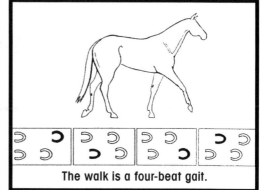

The walk is a four-beat gait.

average stride length of the walk is 5.5 to 6.5 feet.

The trot is considered to be a "two-beat gait" in which the

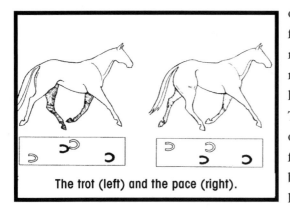

The trot (left) and the pace (right).

opposite hind foot and fore foot hit the ground simultaneously, e.g., the right forelimb and the left hindlimb move together. The average stride length of the trot is nine to 17 feet. The pace is a two-beat gait in which the hind foot and fore foot on the same side hit the ground simultaneously.

The canter has three beats in which the non-leading forelimb and the opposite hindlimb strike the ground at the same time. For example, if the horse is cantering on the left lead, the right

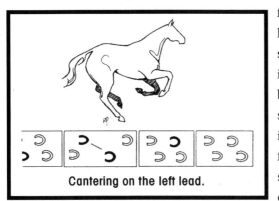

Cantering on the left lead.

forelimb and the left hindlimb strike the ground simultaneously. The gallop is a fully extended "four-beat gait" in which the stride length approaches its maximum of 15 to 22 feet or greater. The gait is similar to the canter except that the non-leading forelimb and the opposite hindlimb do not strike the ground together. In this gait there is a period of "suspension" in which all four feet are off the ground at the same time.

EXAMPLES OF DEVIATIONS IN THE WAY OF GOING:

Winging — The flight of the foot goes through an inner arc when advancing and might cause interference with the opposite forelimb (usually seen with a horse that toes out whether it is base-narrow or base-wide).

Plaiting — The foot travels an inward arc and lands more or less directly in front of the opposite forefoot. (Usually seen with base narrow, toed-out conformation.)

Paddling — An outward deviation of the foot during flight (usually seen with a horse that toes in whether he is base-narrow or base-wide).

Scalping — The toe of the front foot hits the hair-line at the coronary band or above on the hind foot of the same side. Generally a fault of the trotting horse.

Forging — The toe of the hind foot hits the sole area of the forefoot on the same side.

Over-reaching — The toe of the hind foot catches the forefoot on the same

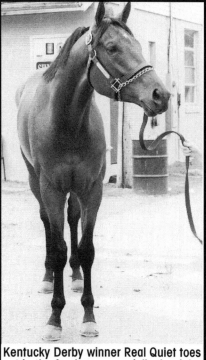

Kentucky Derby winner Real Quiet toes out in the forelegs, especially the right.

side, usually on the heel (may cause shoe pulling).

Cross-firing — Generally confined to pacers and consists of contact on the inside of the diagonal fore and hind feet.

Interfering — Occurs both in front and hind feet. It is a striking, anywhere between the coronary band and the cannon, by the opposite foot which is in motion.

Speedy cutting — Any type of limb interference in the fast gait.

Brushing — A general term for light striking, especially as in forging or interfering.

Elbow hitting — When the horse hits the elbow with the shoe of the same limb (especially with weighted shoes).

Knee hitting — A case of high interference, generally seen in Standardbreds.

CHAPTER 7

Musculoskeletal System and Common Problems

The structure, form, and function of the horse's body represent an amazing creation. All of the body systems work in complete symmetry and synchronization to provide the horse with power and grace. Working in concert, these systems allow the horse to perform, jump, eat, and simply exist. The better these systems are understood the better you can understand how they interact to create the wondrous horse. In addition, the better you understand these body systems the better you will be at taking care of them. Early recognition of problems within the body systems allows for the early recognition of disease processes. The earlier such problems are identified, the better the chances of correcting many of them.

THE MUSCULOSKELETAL SYSTEM

The musculoskeletal system is a complicated network of hundreds of bones, muscles, tendons, and ligaments all working together to produce an animal of great strength, grace, and beauty.

Muscles are the super strong tissues that allow horses to have all of the characteristics that we desire in an athlete. They enable horses to jump six-foot fences, gallop 35 miles an hour for a mile and a quarter, perform complicated yet precise movements, and trot or canter for 100 miles. Of course, probably the same horse could not perform every activity perfectly, but that's why there is such diversity in horse breeds. All horses have the same anatomical muscles, but muscle type often dictates what athletic activity in which a breed of horse will excel. For example, the slim and petite Arabian breed is known for its stamina at long distances, and Arabian horses in

---

AT A GLANCE

- Horses can suffer from a wide variety of muscle sorenesses.

- A veterinarian should evaluate muscle soreness to rule out a more serious problem.

- Alternative therapies such as acupuncture can help treat and reduce muscle pain.

- Tendonitis results from excessive stress which tears tendon fiber bundles.

---

general dominate at endurance rides. The Quarter Horse, with its massive, muscular hindquarters, would be able to blow away any Arabian at a short distance. However, at a distance of 50 miles, the Quarter Horse will be far behind the Arabian. It is amazing how the horse has adapted and the different breeds have excelled at very different sports.

This difference in performance within the same species is due to the development of breeds by selecting for certain traits (i.e., heavy muscle for short bursts of speed or pulling heavy machinery, lighter muscles for speed and fine motor control). Breeds of horses and muscle types, however, do not always dictate the ability of a horse to perform a certain activity. Many variations within a breed exist and the muscles of horses greatly adapt with training. So, just because a horse is a certain breed does not mean it is suited only for certain activities.

What are the muscle types?

Skeletal muscles cover the bones and produce movement when they contract, as compared to smooth muscles which are found, for example, with the intestines and are responsible for moving ingesta through the gastrointestinal tract. It makes sense that these two different types of muscles have very different strength and metabolic requirements.

Muscles are made up of many small fibers. These fibers are arranged into bundles. There are many bundles that come together to make up a muscle.

Muscles are often described by categorizing them into one of three types. A type I muscle fiber also is referred to as a slow twitch fiber, twitch being the contraction followed by relaxation of the muscle fiber. It has a slow speed of contraction and the fibers are small in diameter. There is also a type II a and II b. These fiber types are both fast twitch, with type II b being the fastest. The fiber type an individual possesses is controlled not only by genetics, but by gender. Of course, training can influence the development of type II fibers. When horses are exercising at an easy pace, say a jog, type I fibers within the muscles are used predominately with some of type II a fibers. As the speed or duration of exercise increases, then so does the demand for more muscle fibers to participate in the movement. Type II b fibers are used only at very fast speeds, such as in racing Thoroughbreds or in endurance horses which have been jogging for several hours.

MUSCLE SORENESS OR PAIN

Have you ever had a really hard workout at the gym or run a few extra miles because you felt really good or participated in a long road race? What did you feel like the next day? If you have experienced this type of pain or soreness, then you should have some insight into the pain horses can feel when their muscles are sore. Muscle soreness is being recognized more and more as a cause of poor performance and lameness in horses.

There is a wide variation in muscle soreness in horses. The pain can vary from just mild soreness, recognized as stiffness in a horse's movements, that you see the day following a very hard workout to the severe pain that occurs with exertional rhabdomyolysis ("tying-up"). With this type of severe muscle pain, the horse can be reluctant to move, have swelling in the hindquarter muscles, and can appear colicky, with profuse sweating. In very severe cases, the horse can become recumbent. Traumatic injuries such as muscle tears also can result in only a mild stiffness or shortness of stride to a severe, crippling lameness, depending on the muscle that is damaged.

Muscle pain or soreness can cause lameness but more commonly it is a source of poor performance. A chronically injured muscle can nag at a horse, which cannot tell you, "Gee, when I take off for the jump my back muscles just kill me." What you experience is a horse which is in long-term pain and eventually will refuse to jump or change leads, etc.

Muscle pain is more difficult to diagnose than other, more obvious sources of poor performance, such as the loud noises heard from an upper airway problem like roaring or a head-bobbing lameness. Poor performance, for example in racehorses, could be due to "slow disease" which is just the horse's inability to perform as we would like it. Simply put, the horse has intrinsic physical limitations which will not allow it to be a champion.

WHAT MAKES MUSCLES SORE?

Now, let's explore why muscles hurt. During exercise, injury to muscle cells can cause early fatigue and pain. Injury could be in the form of overexertion, muscle tearing, or exertional myopathy. Overexertion is just that — exercise in excess of what the horse is used to, be it racing, jumping, or pulling. The horse is usually stiff the following day and palpation of the affected muscles reveals a tight band of muscles, instead of supple and soft as they normally feel. The muscles respond painfully to palpation and can be swollen.

Muscle tears also can cause marked pain and/or lameness, and can result from fatigue. As a horse tires, the muscles are more prone to damage as they become less elastic. When the muscle fibers are damaged, there is pain from the resulting inflammation of the torn fibers. If a blood vessel is damaged from within the muscle, then a hematoma will form, causing pressure on the surrounding tissue and pain.

Muscle strain can be the result of a fall, tripping, and/or twisting of a leg, neck, or the muscles of the back. Muscle strain also varies in severity and might not manifest itself for a day or so.

Strenuous exercise can cause muscle pain.

Horses also might have secondary muscle pain, especially if they have a primary musculoskeletal problem. A classic example is a horse with a chronic primary hindlimb lameness. The lameness might be discrete enough not to be obvious to the owner; however, the horse feels it and compensates by stiffening the back (epaxial muscles). Eventually, the back soreness becomes the most noticeable problem. Treatment of the primary problem, however, will not make the muscle pain resolve spontaneously. The horse will need to be treated for both the primary and secondary problems to become pain-free.

Muscle soreness in horses can and should be evaluated by a veterinarian in the early stages to rule out a more serious problem such as exertional rhabdomyolysis or "tying-up." One hallmark of tying-up is myoglobinuria. Myoglobinuria occurs when the horse's damaged muscles release myoglobin into the blood stream. When this happens, the kidney excretes the myoglobin and it turns the horse's urine brown or red-brown. This is an emergency because the myoglobin can cause severe kidney damage and result in renal failure without treatment. Treatment consists of intravenous fluids and anti-inflammatories such as Banamine. The myoglobinuria might occur only with a severe case of tying-up and the disease can recur in a less severe form, leading to chronic muscle pain. A veterinary examination also can rule out any other serious injury to the tendons or ligaments which might warrant a period of rest or additional medical treatment.

Muscle pain is a fact of life for most human athletes. They deal with the wear and tear placed upon their muscles and joints on a daily basis. Equine athletes are no different. In the past, most veterinarians would recommend drugs to calm inflammation and pain from hurting muscles. The use of anti-inflammatory drugs is still the gold standard in the early post-injury phase to quiet inflammation and encourage rapid healing. However, long-term drug therapy is not always a safe alternative as non-steroidal anti-inflammatories have gastrointestinal and/or renal side effects. Furthermore, the drugs, which are used as a quick fix to calm muscle inflammation, could mask the problem temporarily. Once drug therapy ends, the problem can rear its ugly head again. Furthermore, drugs such as anti-inflammatories have restricted use or are banned from horses during most competitions.

ALTERNATIVE THERAPIES

Acupuncture

Acupuncture is an ancient technique used by the Chinese for thousands of years and still in use today. Only within the last few decades has it gained some acceptance within the medical and veterinary fields, so not all medical professionals approve of its use. However, more and more veterinarians are using this technique to diagnose and treat diseases in the horse. The very basic principle of acupuncture lies in the belief that there is a constant energy flow through the body (called Chi), and when this is interrupted, there is 'dis-ease' and this is manifested in a physical form. Energy flows through channels in the body, where the acupuncture points are located. In acupuncture, needles can stimulate these points. In veterinary medicine, depositing saline or vitamin B12 in these points often can cause longer term stimulation. Stimulating acupuncture points resets or restores the energy flow and therefore restores health. This is a very simplified explanation for a very complex and not completely understood modality.

Chiropractic examination

There is much confusion surrounding chiropractic work in horses. This confusion has led to the rejection of the idea of chiropractic manipulations by veterinarians as effective treatments for muscle pain in horses. The terminology used in chiropractics also has been confusing and has led to misun-

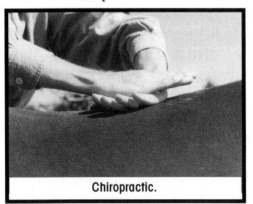

Chiropractic.

derstandings, such as "adjusting" a horse. An "adjustment" is placing a force over a joint or vertebrae to stretch the joint, subsequently releasing tension in the soft tissues surrounding a joint. This "adjustment" is not meant as putting bones back into place as so often is misinterpreted. Stretching a joint often allows relaxation of the surrounding tissues, alleviating muscle pain and/or spasms. Repeated treatment can be used to treat chronic muscle pain successfully in performance horses. I cannot stress enough the importance of having a veterinarian perform the chiropractic examination. An "adjustment" made on a sore horse without a diagnosis can lead to fractures or serious muscle damage. Furthermore, the unique equine anatomy makes it difficult for a non-veterinarian to understand his task completely or to be effective in treatment.

Massage therapy

Equine massage therapy is one of the fastest growing

"hands-on" therapies. Massage is a technique using the hands, fingers, elbows, or other instruments to stimulate soft tissues, usually muscles. Massaging the muscles and other soft tissue structures increases circulation and aids in relaxation of tight, painful muscles. Massage aids in the loosening and stretching of other connective tissues such as fascial layers or joint capsules. It can increase the suppleness and flexibility of muscles when used in conjunction with stretching. Massage also is used in rehabilitation of soft tissue injuries. Combined with stretching, it can help break down adhesions or scar tissue. In humans, a massage also can be profoundly relaxing. Massage should not be used after an acute injury — at least for 48 to 72 hours, to allow for the initial healing process.

Stretching

Up until now, we have focused mainly on the therapies to help horses once an injury or painful condition has occurred. In the last decade, people have started to recognize the benefit of stretching horses' muscles before and after exercise to prevent injury. Human athletes, of course, have been using stretching techniques for decades during warm-up to prepare their muscles and cardiovascular system for work. Stretching also helps prevent painful contractions (spasms) during the cool down. If it works for humans, there is no reason not to believe it can help horses. During the warm-up period, horses can be taken through stretching exercises which can involve flexion and extension of the neck, head, and limbs to better prepare their muscles to work. However, stretching can be harmful if used improperly. Cold muscles can be over-stretched, leading to small tears within the muscles. These small tears can be painful and result in scar tissue within the muscles. Never pull on your horse's legs, well-known equine therapist Mimi Porter advises in her book *The New Equine Sports Therapy*, and always beware of overflexing and overextending your horse's legs while

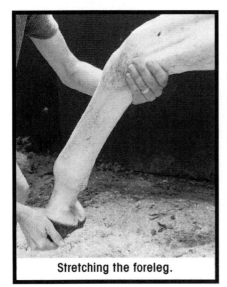

Stretching the foreleg.

stretching. She recommends that before performing any stretching exercises you should talk to your veterinarian about normal mobility and range of motion of horses' muscles and joints to prevent inadvertent injury.

There are many other modalities used to treat and prevent pain in performance horses. They include magnets, therapeutic ultrasound, hydrotherapy, and trigger-point therapy along with acupressure. Discuss the options with your veterinarian to decide which is most likely to help your horse and its particular injury.

TENDON INJURIES

Tendon injuries can be extremely frustrating problems. The best approach is to make every effort to prevent them or limit the degree of damage that occurs. Certainly some acute tendon injuries occur without any warning signs, but many more severe injuries can be preceded by subtle lameness or palpable abnormalities in the tendons. It therefore is important to learn something about tendon structure and function and to perform a basic examination of the tendons to avoid exercising a horse with a potential or developing tendon problem.

ANATOMY AND FUNCTION

The structure and function of a horse's lower leg is beautiful, amazing, somewhat perplexing, and downright complicated. The first thing to understand is the difference between a tendon and a ligament. A tendon is defined as "a fibrous cord of connective tissue continuous with the fibers of a muscle and attaching the muscle to bone or cartilage" — a muscle-to-bone connection. A ligament is defined as "a band of tissue connecting bone or cartilage, serving to support and strengthen joints" — a bone-to-bone connection. Tendons and ligaments are composed of the densest form of fibrous connective tissue, consisting of parallel bundles of coarse, collagen fibers. Collagen is a protein substance that makes up many of the body's connective tissues, including skin and subcutaneous tissue as well as tendons. The simplified difference between the collagen in the elastic tissue of the skin and that in a tendon is the degree of organization of the collagen fibers. In the skin, the collagen fibers are loosely arranged and do not have much "strength," whereas in the tendon the collagen fibers are very tightly organized in a parallel manner, providing a significant increase in strength.

Tendons have great tensile strength. Tensile strength refers to the resistance of a material to a force that tends to tear it apart when it is stretched or extended. In addition to their strength, tendons have the property of elasticity — they are capable of absorbing and storing energy when stretched. The concept of an object other than a battery that "stores" energy was always a tough one for me in physics class. But the analogy that always stuck with me was one of those little balsa wood airplanes with the plastic propeller and a rubber band for an engine. The wound up (stretched) elastic rubber band has absorbed the kinetic energy of stretching it and stored it as potential energy. This elastic recoil of tendons is thought by many to contribute substantially to locomotion. The forces applied to the foreleg of an exercising horse are greatest at impact as can be seen by the classic "dropping" of the fetlock of a racing Thoroughbred. Under these forces the tendons on the back of the legs are "absorbing" the impact by stretching. During mid-stride, the force decreases, then rapidly increases again as the leg "pushes" off the ground. During this phase of movement, energy "stored" in the tendons due to their stretching is released and contributes to locomotion.

The tendons of the legs consist of two groups: the flexors and extensors. Both the flexors and extensors have their muscle body residing on the forearm above the carpus (knee) or hock. The extensors are on the dorsal (front) surface of the leg and function in extending the leg and in weight bearing. If all the extensor tendons were dysfunctional, the limb would not be held straight in extension to support weight and the leg would collapse at the carpus under weight or drag the toe when the limb was in motion.

There are five extensor tendons of the forearm with the main one being called the common digital extensor tendon which travels the entire length of the leg and attaches to the top part of the coffin bone. Another significant tendon of the forearm is the extensor carpi radialis. This tendon inserts in the cannon bone just under the carpus. Both can be felt as a firm, roughly half-centimeter-thick structure just under the skin with the extensor carpi radialis being felt best just above the carpus and the common digital extensor tendon being felt best on the dorsal surface of the cannon bone.

The flexor group resides on the back (plantar) surface of the leg and functions in flexing the leg, absorbing the forces applied to the leg in motion, assisting in the support of the leg when weight bearing, and assisting in locomotion. The two flexor tendons are the superficial digital flexor and the deep digital flexor that course the back surface of the cannon bone and insert on the pastern bones and the coffin bone, respectively.

An additional structure associated with many tendons in

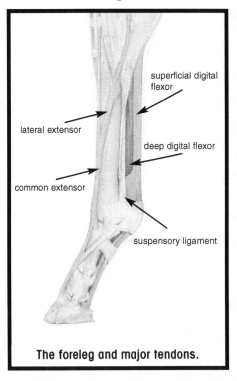

lateral extensor

superficial digital flexor

deep digital flexor

common extensor

suspensory ligament

The foreleg and major tendons.

certain areas is the tendon "sheath." The tendon sheath is just that: a sheath of tissue that surrounds the tendon. Within the sheath there is a very small quantity of a viscous fluid that acts as a "lubricant" in areas where the tendon glides. The main tendon sheath of interest surrounds both the superficial and deep digital flexor tendons in roughly the upper third and lower third of the tendon bodies, with the middle (near the center of the cannon bone) having no sheath. Distension of the lower digital flexor tendon sheath is typically called a common "wind puff."

When viewing the side of the leg in a standing, weight-bearing horse, three structures can be seen in the mid-cannon bone region from front to back: the cannon bone, the suspensory ligament, and the flexor tendons. There is not much else to the lower leg and these structures are just under the skin. It also should be noted that when the leg is bearing weight, the tendons are often perceived to be as hard as the cannon bone due to the tension forces applied to them during weight bearing. The best way to feel the flexor tendons (and the suspensory ligament) is by picking up the leg. In this posture, the separation between the superficial and deep digital flexor tendon can be detected. Also, note how "soft" the tendons feel when they are not supporting weight.

Now, it gets a little more complicated because there are ligaments associated with the tendons. Both the superficial digital flexor and deep digital flexor have a "check" ligament. The proximal (upper) check ligament originates from the back surface of the radius (the main bone above the carpus) and attaches to the superficial digital flexor tendon, and the distal (lower) check ligament originates off the back of the carpus and attaches to the deep digital flexor tendon. These check ligaments support what is called the passive stay apparatus. Because of the fetlock's angle, much of the weight coming down each leg is supported by the suspensory ligament as well as the superficial and deep digital flexor tendons. If the suspensory ligament and flexor tendons were severed, the fetlock would drop to the ground. The check ligaments create a "bypass" between the muscle in the upper leg and its tendons' insertion in the lower leg. If the muscles were entirely responsible for assisting in fetlock support at rest, they would soon fatigue. The check ligament creates a direct, dense, connective link between the bones of the forearm and the foot via the flexor tendons. The check ligaments can be an individual source of lameness as they, too, can suffer injury. Surgically manipulating one of the check ligaments can help treat some tendon injuries.

EXAMINATION OF TENDONS

The most common causes of forelimb lameness generally trace to the foot. Foot abscesses, for instance, occasionally make the leg swollen and painful, so the foot always should be ruled out first. Anytime there is overt lameness, especially in the forelimbs, the tendons should be evaluated if there is no other obvious cause. Also, I generally like to perform daily examination of the flexor tendons on horses in heavy training or those stepping up in difficult work. In addition, certain kinds of footing, such as heavy, deep, or uneven, can predispose to tendon injury, so if a horse starts working on such footing, I also like to keep track of what's going on in the tendons. Not all horses with early tendon injury show overt signs of lameness. When I groomed show horses in Florida, we would always pay more attention to tendons when the horses started exercising more in the deep sand footing — especially horses with a history of tendon problems.

The easiest tendon injuries to diagnose are the ones that have a gross enlargement of the tendon and have the appearance of the classic "bowed" tendon. In these horses, the tendon is sore to touch and the horse is generally quite lame, but more subtle injury can be much more difficult to diagnose.

As with any other type of tissue damage the hallmarks of inflammation are heat, pain, and swelling. After noting if any of these are present, a veterinarian usually picks up the leg and conducts a very careful, methodical palpation of each tendon. With experience, one can tell if a tendon is enlarged or thicker than normal which might go along with an acute or chronic injury depending on whether the enlargement is edema/inflammation or a build up of scar tissue. Also determine if firmly squeezing the tendon causes consistent pain and to what degree. This is where experience comes into play. It is not uncommon for many horses in a moderate to heavy training program to carry some degree of mild sensitivity to palpation of the suspensory ligament and perhaps to a lesser degree in the tendons. If the pain is excessive, is associated with lameness, or is markedly different between the two legs, it is most likely significant.

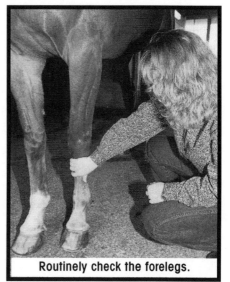
Routinely check the forelegs.

How much sensitivity is too much? That's a tough question to answer, especially when many tendon injuries are most likely a collection of minor traumas that add up to a serious injury. The one thing for certain is that if there is some injury to the tendons, and the horse continues to train, the injury most likely will worsen. If you suspect tendon damage, seek veterinary assessment.

The most useful diagnostic tool for tendon examination is ultrasound. The use of ultrasonography has become commonplace in the objective evaluation of suspected tendon and ligament injury. The size of the tendon lesions can be assessed to help determine how much of the total tendon diameter is abnormal. Ultrasound also can assess the degree of abnormality within the tendon fiber structure. In addition, ultrasonography can provide a permanent record of the injury at a specific point in time and allow for direct comparison. The serial ultrasonography of a damaged tendon monitors the healing response and can help determine when the horse can safely return to work.

TENDON INJURY

Tendon injury can occur because of external trauma such as a leg being caught under a plank (or even due to a slipped bandage) or mechanical overload. It is appropriate to call most tendon injuries a tendonitis (the suffix -itis indicating inflammation). It is commonly agreed that tendonitis results from excessive stress which stretches and ruptures the tendon fiber bundles. This can happen "all at once" if there is a single and massive stress applied to the tendons, such as an extreme misstep on irregular footing at high speed or stepping into a woodchuck hole. But most cases of tendonitis are thought to result from an "additive" effect of previous and repetitive low-grade tendon fiber disruption. Each repetitive stress causes minor disruption or tearing of the tendon fibers. This damage causes some inflammation in the area and edema within and around the tendon as well as the production of inflammatory enzymes that further damage the collagen fibers of the tendon. The net result of the inflammation created by the tendon fiber tearing is a series of events that further damage and weaken the surrounding tendon fibers.

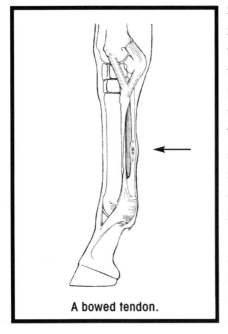

A bowed tendon.

Factors that have been implicated in the development of flexor tendonitis include increased tendon stresses from uneven and deep track surfaces, muscle fatigue from

During a pre-purchase or lameness exam, it is important to watch the horse move (above); the veterinarian below is checking for any neurological problems by watching placement of the feet.

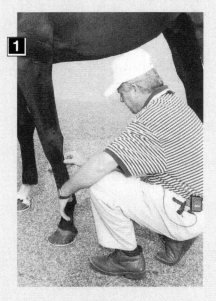

1) Checking the tendons;
2) examining the shoulder;
3) palpating the back muscles.

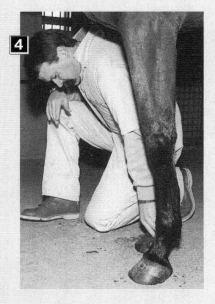

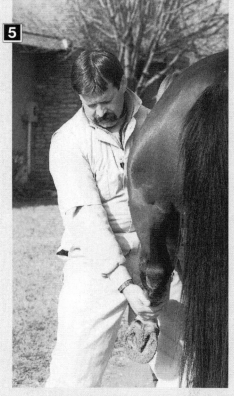

4) Checking the digital pulse;

5) a flexion test of a hind leg;

6) using the hoof testers to check for any sensitivity in the feet.

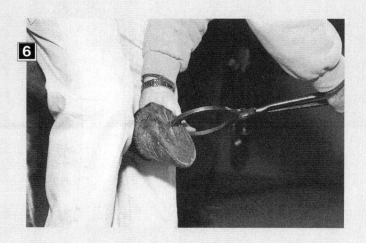

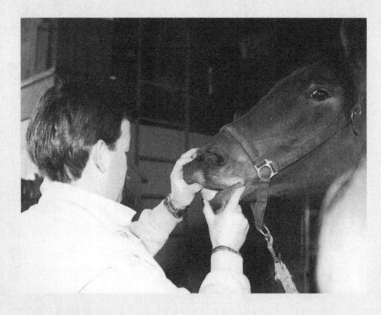

Checking the capillary refill time (above) in which the gum is pressed, then released; (below) the veterinarian is examining this horse's back teeth.

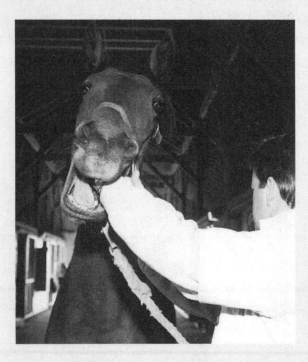

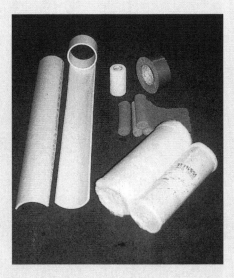

Materials for a splint (above) include piping, cotton bandages, elastic wrap, and duct tape; (below) the author demonstrating the proper application of a splint.

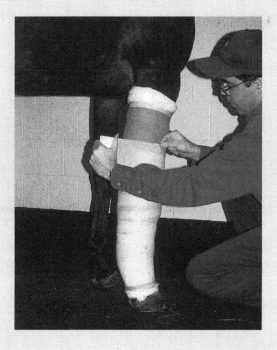

The horse above is acting "off," a sign of a potential problem; below, a horse with tetanus (lockjaw). Note the hay in its mouth.

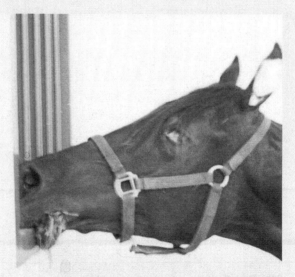

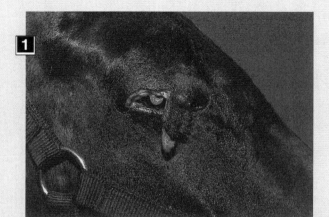

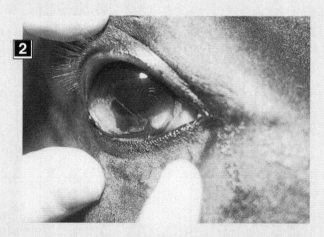

1) A horse with an eye lid laceration;
2) a fungal ulcer;
3) a severe bacterial ulcer.

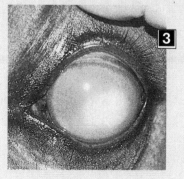

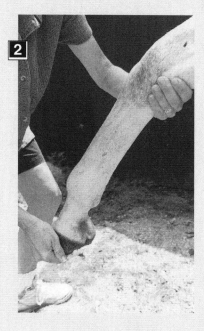

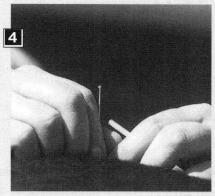

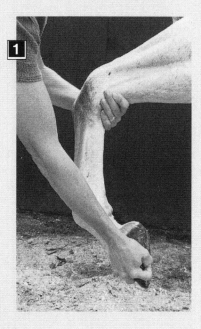

Alternative therapies:
stretching (1 & 2);
electrical stimulation (3);
and acupuncture (4).

poor or inadequate training, excessively long toes and long sloping pasterns, and poorly applied bandages or boots.

It is also important to mention again that not all horses with subtle tendon or ligament damage will show overt signs of lameness. This fact is unfortunate, as repetitive low grade injury most likely occurs and goes unnoticed in the period preceding a serious tendon injury. This fact is one reason why intense veterinary inspections prior to three-day eventing, higher level show jumping, and racing have helped greatly in preventing catastrophic breakdown injuries. Tendons and suspensory ligaments are of special focus during these inspections.

SUPERFICIAL DIGITAL FLEXOR TENDON

The superficial digital flexor tendon is the tendon most commonly affected with tendonitis and is particularly common in Thoroughbred racehorses, although, as many of you unfortunately might know from personal experience, any breed performing almost any discipline can develop tendonitis. The distribution of common forelimb injuries has been reported in Thoroughbreds while racing on dirt surfaces. A study looked at 1,039 Thoroughbreds in 15 different states and reported that 139 (13.4%) of Thoroughbreds racing that year had experienced a bowed tendon/tendonitis. This was the most common injury reported in this study.

Superficial digital flexor tendonitis most commonly affects the forelimb, but is seen occasionally in the hindlimb. Thoroughbreds racing in the United States (counter clockwise), more commonly develop superficial digital flexor tendonitis in the left front leg, presumably due to a greater stress applied to the inside leg. In performance horses competing in other activities, superficial digital flexor tendonitis has an equal incidence with respect to which foreleg develops it. Tendonitis does occur in the deep digital flexor tendon, but is much less common.

THERAPY

The treatment is very much the same regardless of the tendon involved. The basic principals are to reduce the inflammation and stress on the tendon and therefore minimize the damage, accurately assess the degree of damage so a therapeutic plan/prognosis and rehabilitation program can be established, and allow adequate rest time for healing.

The first step, regardless if it is an acute tendonitis or an acute manifestation of a more chronic tendonitis, is to control the inflammation. If you suspect tendonitis, the application of cold as soon as possible is a good first move. This can be accomplished via ice boots, ice towels, a manure bucket full of ice water, a number of new frostily numbing gizmos on the commercial equine market, or the faithful standby — the cold water hose. One of my personal favorites, mostly because I'm cheap, is a rubber inner tube for a truck tire filled with ice water (after being placed on the leg) and taped on above the carpus. Regardless of your choice of weapon for cold application, one important point is that it is possible to overdo it.

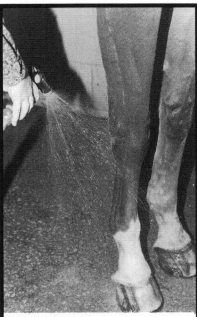

Hosing can reduce inflammation.

One of the major benefits of cold is that it constricts the blood vessels and thereby slows down the movement of inflammation-creating blood cells into the damaged area. But if the cold is applied for too long (generally greater than 20 minutes), the rest of the tissue in the area senses that there is not enough blood supply. Those blood vessels dilate, which can negate the beneficial effects of the cold therapy. The most benefit from cold therapy probably comes from 20-minute applications spaced several hours apart. The cold therapy usually is maintained for three to five days after discovery of the injury. In between cold treatments, the leg should be placed under firm pressure by a heavy support bandage. The pressure places a counter force that potentially reduces edema formation in and around the damaged tendon. The application of antiphlogistic or other type poultices can be applied (not hot!) for longer time periods in between cold treatments.

In reality, a support bandage does not significantly reduce the tensile forces applied to the tendon while weight bearing. In some cases of severe tendon damage, the application of a cast for several weeks followed by the use of a fetlock support shoe may be warranted.

Use of anti-inflammatory drugs, such as phenylbutazone, also can reduce/limit inflammation. Always find out why your horse is lame before treating with anti-inflammatory drugs, which can mask the pain. It is especially important not to exercise the horse if a tendon injury is suspected as continued exercise, especially if pain-relieving medication has been given, can cause further damage. Long-term

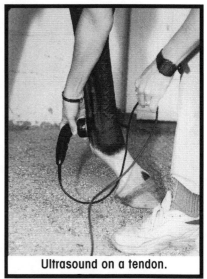

Ultrasound on a tendon.

rest with an extremely regimented exercise program is in the future for most horses with a moderate tendonitis.

Before discussing other current and experimental treatment options it is important to mention how tendons heal. Remember back in the structure and function section the tendon was described as a bundle of collagen fibers highly organized in a parallel manner. It is that specific structure that provides the tensile strength and elasticity that dictates the parameters and limits of tendon function. When the highly organized tendon fiber structure is disrupted by tendonitis (or laceration, tearing, etc.), it will never be the same again. As the tendon heals, the new tissue is of a different type collagen and does not easily recreate the organized structure necessary for completely normal function. The scar tissue that forms is not as strong as normal tendon tissue and could be subject to recurrent tendonitis when the animal is placed back into training. Now with that gloomy statement out of the way, we can talk about currently known ways to maximize the strength of healing tendon tissue and several procedures that have been shown to limit recurrence of tendonitis.

For minor tendonitis the previously mentioned therapies and a prescribed period of rest could be all that is necessary, but if the tendon injury is graded as moderate to severe and/or the horse is a serious performance horse, additional treatment options might be necessary — especially considering the potential for recurrence.

TENDON "SPLITTING"

If there is a large "core" type lesion seen on the ultrasound, a tendon splitting procedure often is performed. These "core" lesions represent an area of severe disruption of tendon fibers and a collection of blood, edema fluid, and devitalized tissue. The simplified goal is to open these core lesions up to the surface of the tendon, allowing their contents to drain out and potentially let in a new blood supply. The procedure can be performed with the horse standing under heavy sedation or under general anesthesia in combination with the next procedure we'll talk about. In short, the leg is aseptically prepared for surgery and, with the aid of ultrasound, a "stab" incision is made with a small scalpel blade through the skin, tendon, and directly into the core lesion. It has been demonstrated that the splitting of acute to subacute cases of tendonitis, which possessed core lesions, led to a significant decrease in lesion size and tendon diameter (based on ultrasonography) within eight to 12 days after surgery.

When these cases were followed over time, there was an obvious decrease in the tendon diameter, presumably due to a decreased deposition of scar tissue. Additional research has shown that 81% of horses returned to performance with 68% competing at the same level of performance. Other studies have shown that horses with similar lesions treated without tendon splitting had a 50% chance of returning to performance at the same level as prior to the tendon injury.

Remember the check ligament that attaches the superficial digital flexor tendon to the bone of the forearm? A surgical procedure that severs the proximal check ligament (desmotomy) has shown great promise in the treatment of superficial flexor tendonitis.

It is hypothesized that by removing the direct tendon-bone connection, the transection of the proximal ligament allows the muscle belly of the superficial digital flexor tendon to become more supportive and thereby reduce some of the tensile forces placed on the tendon.

An additional medical therapy generally reserved for tendonitis in the area of a tendon sheath is the injection of hyaluronic acid. Hyaluronic acid is often used in the treatment of joint disease and is considered to be a joint "lubricant" with many of its beneficial properties aimed at reducing inflammation. The benefits of hyaluronic acid for the treatment of tendonitis are controversial, but there are some studies that demonstrate a positive effect.

Another medical treatment currently being investigated, although still at the experimental stage, is the injection of tendon lesions with beta-aminopropionitrile (BAPN). BAPN has been shown to reduce scar tissue formation in people. The drug is injected into the tendon lesions and the horses are placed into a rigorous, low-level, controlled exercise program. Results of clinical trials show the horses rapidly become sound and have improved tendon fiber alignment and reduced overall tendon diameter as determined by ultrasound. Long-term data on these horses' return to performance is still being collected.

There is general agreement that for a moderately damaged tendon the first 30 days of therapy, regardless of any of the aforementioned therapeutic interventions, should consist mainly of stall rest, with possible daily hand walking for 15 to 30 minutes, depending on your veterinarian's advice. The next phase of therapy, and usually the most difficult for many horse owners to accept, consists mainly of rest and controlled exercise for a significant period of time after injury.

Depending on the degree of severity, most horses still will require six to 10 months before recommencing training. Typical aftercare for a horse after a proximal check ligament desmotomy can consist of two to four weeks of stall rest, six weeks of hand walking, and eight weeks of light jogging or pasture exercise. Another rehabilitation regimen for a horse with a moderate tendonitis consists of initial stall confinement with 15 to 30 minutes of hand walking for the first month. For the second month, hand walking is increased to 45 minutes per day. For the third month, 20 minutes walking with a rider up or 10 minutes of swimming per day can be attempted. After the third month, gradually increased walking with a rider up or riderless ponying is good with most being able to be cantered after five months. Many can go back into light work at nine months.

Studies have shown that rehabilitation consisting of a gradually building exercise program promotes better healing of the tendon and could reduce the chance of recurrence when the horse eventually resumes full training. All along the way the progress of the healing can be followed with ultrasonography, with the rehabilitation program adjusted if necessary. The continued and careful monitoring of the rehabilitation program is essential to prevent re-injury.

Obviously each horse and each injury have to be treated as individuals. A treatment program and rehabilitation regimen have to be based on the severity of the tendon lesion as determined by veterinary examination and ultrasonography, the current use of the horse, the future desired use of the horse, the economic ability of the individual owner, and the owner's commitment and patience to the horse's rehabilitation. For some minor tendon injuries in pleasure horses, the horse can be treated and returned to that level of activity in as short as a few months. A moderate to severe injury requires extensive management and can take up to a year of rehabilitation before the horse can return to work with minimized risk of re-injury.

CHAPTER 8

The Foot

The old saying goes "no foot, no horse," and as clichés go, this is a good one. The horse's foot is a unique structure that can be a source of significant problems. This chapter will give an overview of the foot and related problems. For more detailed information, read *Understanding Laminitis* and *Understanding the Equine Foot*, both part of The Horse Health Care Library series.

Before shoeing your horse, have your farrier and veterinarian devise a plan based on the horse's use, conformation, environment, and any pre-existing problems. There are many fads and unfortunately many of the things we do to our horses are not dictated by common sense. I am a minimalist and believe that simple solutions and sound basics are the way to go for most horses. A problem might require

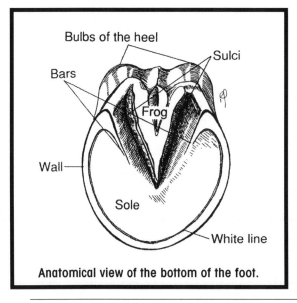

Bulbs of the heel

Sulci

Bars

Frog

Wall

Sole

White line

Anatomical view of the bottom of the foot.

a special shoe, but using something just because it is a fad is generally wrong. Your horse (and its feet) is an individual and should be treated as such.

The foot is designed to maintain a relatively perfect balance of hydration (hard and dehydrated on the outside and soft and hydrated on the inside) if it is not exposed to environmental extremes. The balance of water within the foot is important so the hard keratin shell can maintain flexibility to allow shock absorption and heal expansion when bearing full weight.

AT A GLANCE

- Work with your farrier and vet to devise a shoeing plan.

- Too much moisture is bad for a horse's feet.

- Neglected feet, muddy pastures, and dirty stalls can contribute to or cause thrush.

- Laminitis is an inflammation of the sensitive tissue inside the foot. It can be caused by grain overload or a number of other factors.

There are numerous products on the market that propose to soften, harden, moisturize, seal the moisture in, etc. Most of these products have not undergone controlled scientific experiments and many of them, in my personal experience, do either nothing or the opposite of what is proclaimed. Be careful when choosing these products and seek professional recommendation.

The environment plays a big role in foot health. I think the greater danger comes from an environment that is too wet. This type of environment is a breeding ground for the organisms that cause thrush, canker, and white line disease in addition to making the soft tissue of the frog potentially more susceptible to these infections. It is important to make an effort to provide some dry footing if you are stuck with a wet, soggy environment. Some areas like this can benefit from being clean filled with dirt or gravel. If you are stuck with a wet environment, the daily care of the feet is more important. The feet should be picked out at least twice a day and evaluated for signs of infection so if treatment is necessary, it can be started early. It also pays to keep stalls clean and extra dry as a mucky stall also can contribute to foot problems.

THRUSH

One of the more common problems affecting the feet is thrush. Thrush is most likely a bacterial infection of the crevices of the frog and can become severe enough to cause lameness. The major predisposing factors are poor hygiene, poor hygiene, and poor hygiene. This is related to both the environment and lack of adequate cleaning of the foot. If the horse is stabled, poor stall cleaning techniques can be a contributing factor. In addition, wet and mucky paddocks can predispose to thrush.

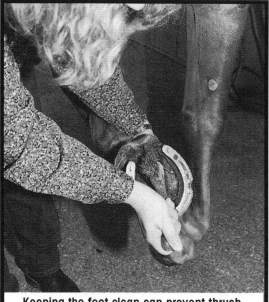

Keeping the foot clean can prevent thrush.

Clinical signs include a foul smelling odor emanating from the foot when it is cleaned out, an excessively soft and/or painful frog with a black and necrotic texture to it (these can occasionally be so bad the frog will bleed).

The main part of treatment is to have your farrier trim away all of the dead and infected tissue and to maintain the cleanliness of the foot. Depending on the severity, your farrier and/or veterinarian might recommend a variety of treatments. A word of caution on the many over-the-counter/homemade remedies. I think almost any of these will work as the important part is cleaning the foot and maintaining it in a clean environment. Excessive use of almost any treatment can do more harm than good. Most are relatively caustic chemicals which can exacerbate the soreness if used in excess. Remember to follow the directions or advice of your farrier/veterinarian.

FOOT PUNCTURES/ABSCESSES

If a single foot is warm and there is sensitivity around the coronary band and/or an increased pulse, the likely cause is a foot abscess. The bottom surface of the foot should be evaluated for any foreign objects, such as a nail, if this is not already the obvious cause of the lameness. Should a foreign object have created a puncture wound in the foot it should NOT be removed until a veterinarian has had a chance to evaluate it. If the object is protruding signifi-

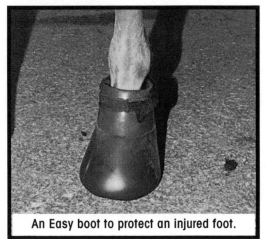

An Easy boot to protect an injured foot.

cantly you can tape some small wooden blocks to the foot or cut the object off close to the foot with wire or bolt cutters to prevent it from going in further. But, again, it should NOT be removed. The reason for leaving the object in the foot is that, depending on the location of the puncture, your veterinarian most likely will want to take a radiograph to determine if deeper structures are involved. The specific location of the puncture can greatly affect the initial treatment plan and the prognosis.

LAMINITIS (FOUNDER)

The word "founder" means "to sink to the ground" and refers to what can happen in the aftermath of an episode of laminitis. The coffin bone actually can become detached from the hoof wall and "sink" toward the ground. Laminitis is a disease process of the feet in which the sensitive laminae which connect the hoof wall to the coffin bone become inflamed. The disease is most common in the front feet, but can affect hind feet and all feet. The pony breeds have an increased suscepti-

bility to laminitis, but horses of all breeds, ages, and disciplines can easily be affected given the appropriate circumstances.

Laminitis is an extremely painful, sometimes fatal condi-

A laminitic horse is reluctant to move.

tion. It can be related to a number of specific risk factors with overeating of grain perhaps the most well known. In fact, the overingestion of carbohydrates, such as grain, could reproduce the disease so predictably it was the accepted scientific method for creating laminitis for research purposes.

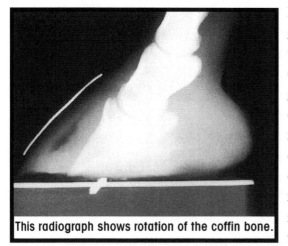

In addition to overeating grain, the sudden ingestion of fresh lush pasture ("grass founder"), the ingestion of large amounts of cold water ("water founder"), the severe concussion of working on a hard surface ("road founder"), the development of a uterine infection related to a retained

This radiograph shows rotation of the coffin bone.

placenta, infection with the causative organism of Potomac horse fever, infection with salmonella, the presence of a pituitary tumor, and a variety of other systemic illnesses are risk factors for the development of laminitis.

All horses and ponies appear to be different in their individual susceptibility to the development of laminitis. It is prudent to ensure that all grain products are secure from those midnight escape artists and that introduction to a fresh, lush, spring pasture is done gradually. If your horse is experiencing any of the other mentioned risk factors, early recognition and treatment can help reduce the chances of developing laminitis.

CHAPTER 9

The Respiratory System

The respiratory system's main goal is to transfer oxygen from the air we breathe to the red blood cells where the oxygen will be transported throughout the body and be available for all organs and tissues. In addition, carbon dioxide, a waste product of metabolism, is eliminated from the body via the lungs. Average room air (at sea level) contains about 21% oxygen, some 70% nitrogen, and the remainder a variety of gases including pollution. So, in fact, the air we typically breathe is not very rich in oxygen. As the altitude gets higher the percentage of oxygen in the air becomes less (the air becomes "thinner").

Red blood cells contain an iron-rich protein called hemoglobin. Oxygen molecules bind to hemoglobin when the red blood cells are in the lungs and are released from the hemoglobin in the tissues. Several factors can affect the red blood cells' ability to bind or release oxygen. For example, iron deficiency can lead to anemia and a reduced oxygen-carrying capacity of the blood. Red maple leaf poisoning in horses causes a change in the hemoglobin that decreases its binding of oxygen, and carbon monoxide toxicity prevents the release of oxygen from hemoglobin. There are numerous other toxins that can have an effect on the binding affinity of oxygen for hemoglobin.

Ways to evaluate the respiratory system include respiratory rate and character of breathing, bearing in mind that there are other things that can have an effect on these parameters. For example, pain can increase the respiratory rate and cause shallow breathing. A good physical examination is required to assess the respiratory system adequately. Is there a nasal discharge and if so what is the content of it — clear thin fluid, thick green snot, thick yellow snot, blood content, foul smelling, one nostril or both? Is there normal air flow out of both nostrils? Is there any asymmetry to the head? Has the horse been coughing and if so what is the character of the cough (dry/wet)? Can a cough be induced by squeezing the windpipe (trachea)? Is the horse extending its head and neck to breathe? Are there any painful swellings around the head? Does the horse make a noise while breathing? (at rest? at work? on inspiration? on expiration?) Does the horse have extra abdominal movement while breathing? Is there a fever? Are there any other horses on the property with similar signs? All of these things must be assessed and can give clues to the specific problem. Other important factors include: travel history, horse's age, vaccination status, time of year, and prior illness.

Respiratory problems are typically classified as upper or lower respiratory. The anatomy of the upper airway is complex, but requires a good understanding to aid in diagnosis and recognition of disease.

Let's start with the nostrils as these are the entry point for air and that ever so precious oxygen. The numerous muscles of the nostrils generate the flaring (dilating) action which

AT A GLANCE

- A thorough examination is needed to properly assess your horse's respiratory system.

- Respiratory diseases fall into two categories: upper or lower respiratory.

- Blocked nasal passages can cause respiratory distress in horses, which are obligate nasal breathers.

- The causes of pneumonia in horses are numerous.

allows for air movement with the least resistance at this point. Occasionally some horses will have small nostrils that don't open well while exercising, affecting airflow and thus performance. There are minor surgical procedures and other interventions to help correct this problem.

Going up the nostrils, there are three passages stacked on top of each other that lead toward the throat. It is possible for these delicate passageways to become inflamed and lead to nasal passage obstruction. Occasionally foreign bodies (plant material, wood, etc.) can become lodged in a nasal passage and cause inflammation/obstruction. It also has been reported that foreign objects such as gauze sponges have purposefully been inserted into these passages. The horse's head has extremely large sinus cavities that drain into the nasal passages. Horses

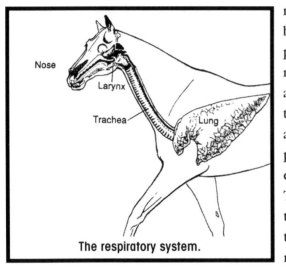

The respiratory system.

have a long nasal septum so that the sinuses drain into the nasal passages on the same side — a nasal discharge only coming from one nostril by sinus drainage.

The next stop on the way toward the back of the throat are the openings to the guttural pouch. The guttural pouch is a structure unique to horses, rhinos, and the Tapir. This structure is an outpouching of the eustachian tube. Whereas our eustachian tube drains from the inner ear to the back of our throat, the horse has a pouch that is fairly large (it holds several hundred milliliters) with the opening draining just behind the nasal septum on each side. A discharge from the guttural pouch can drip down the outer wall of the throat and out the nostril on the same side as the affected pouch, or, if the discharge is great and flowing rapidly, it can come from both nostrils.

The guttural pouch is a unique but somewhat scary structure for several reasons. The interior of the guttural pouch contains important structures that can be affected by guttural pouch disease. There are four major nerves coming directly out of the brain (cranial nerves) that travel on the inside of

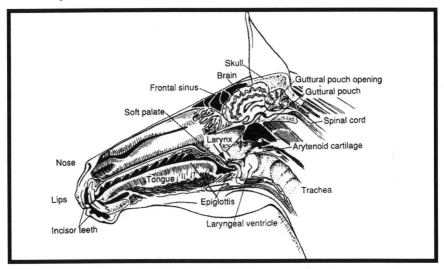

the pouch as well as two major arteries (the internal carotid artery on the way to the brain and the maxillary artery supplying much of the blood to the head). Guttural pouch disease will be discussed further in this chapter.

As we continue on, we come to the voice box or "larynx." Several common disease processes affect airflow in the laryngeal area. In the normal horse, the larynx coordinates swallowing and protects the trachea and thus the lungs from inhalation of feed material. It should be noted at this point that the normal horse cannot breathe through its mouth. Horses are obligate nasal breathers, so anything that occludes the upper airway will cause an airway obstruction and respiratory distress. The laryngeal area is where the soft palate ends (the soft palate separates the oral cavity from the nasal cavity) and the larynx itself is the junction between the nasal cavity and the trachea (windpipe). A triangle-shaped structure called the epiglottis jets out with the point facing forward and sits on top of the soft palate.

As we go fuarther back, just before entering the trachea, there is a V-shaped structure with small bulges on each side called the arytenoids (these are adjacent to the vocal cords and often are called "the flappers"). The arytenoids are pulled open wide during inspiration to allow for maximum unobstructed airflow. There are several problems which occur in this area that we will examine later. Just after going past the arytenoids, we are in the trachea and on the way down to the lungs. Before leaving the head, I want to mention that there are many lymph nodes in the head area that can cause significant problems if they become enlarged.

The windpipe of an adult horse is about three inches in diameter and travels down the center of the neck into the thoracic cavity where it splits into the two main branches just above the heart. The branches of the trachea, now called bronchi, divide many times until all the little (microscopic) branches connect to what is called an "air sac." The air sac is where it all happens. The structure at this level becomes so fine that there is nothing but a single thin membrane separating a single red blood cell from the oxygen in the air sac. It is at this level that the oxygen diffuses across the membrane into the red blood cell and the carbon dioxide diffuses out of the red blood cell and into the air sac to be eliminated when a horse exhales.

The chest or thoracic cavity also can be called the pleural cavity. The "pleura" is the thin, cellular membrane lining the chest cavity (inside of the ribs) and covering the surface of the lungs. Within this cavity the lungs are fully expanded and in close contact with the chest cavity. There is only a very small amount of fluid present within the chest cavity when everything is normal.

FURTHER EVALUATION OF THE RESPIRATORY SYSTEM

There are several other procedures which can be performed to evaluate the respiratory system further. First of all we need to listen to the lungs. With many horses, especially those with an extra inch of fat over their ribs, the lungs can be difficult to hear. It is very useful, since we just can't ask them to take a deep breath, to place a plastic trash bag over the muzzle allowing the horse to rebreathe its expired air for a few minutes.

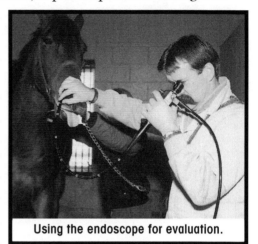

Using the endoscope for evaluation.

The use of a fiberoptic endoscope can greatly assist in evaluating respiratory disease. The upper airway can be directly evaluated, including the sinuses, guttural pouch, and the structures of the larynx. Sometimes it is necessary to evaluate the larynx while the horse is exercising (a task accomplished with the help of a high-speed treadmill). The scope also can be taken well into the lungs to look for abnormal fluid and obtain samples for evaluation and culture.

Should pneumonia or pleuritis be suspected, a transtracheal washing can be performed to collect material for evaluation and culture. Radiology and ultrasonography also can be of great benefit. The head as well as the lungs can be radiographed and ultrasounded. Radiographs of an adult horse's lungs usually can be accomplished only at a referral center with a big machine, but ultrasound examination can be performed easily in the field. In addition, routine blood work also can be useful. With all the background out of the way, I'd like to go through some of the more common respiratory diseases.

NASAL PASSAGES

The nasal passages can be affected by foreign body-induced abscesses caused by everything from small plant awns to pieces of stick several inches long. The clinical signs associated with such problems range from obstruction and reduced air flow in one nostril to the presence of a variety of nasal discharges (clear, yellow/white pus, bloody, etc.). The diagnosis is made using endoscopic examination. More invasive problems in the nasal passages include cancer and fungal infections.

SINUSES

The horse's head is about 50% sinus cavity with the main sinuses being called the "frontal" and the "maxillary." The frontal sinus is in the area between the eyes and to the back of the head and the maxillary sinus is from the eyes down and associated with the teeth. The main connection to the nasal passage is via the maxillary sinus by way of the naso-maxillary opening; the right maxillary sinus drains into the right nasal passage and the left maxillary sinus drains into the left nasal passage. The naso-maxillary opening is about halfway from the nostril to the end of the nasal septum, so drainage from a diseased sinus comes from the nostril on the same side as the affected sinus.

The most common cause of a sinus infection in the horse results from an infected tooth root. The average horse has six pairs (one top and one bottom) of cheek teeth on each side. There are three premolars and three molars with an occasional horse having an additional premolar often referred to as a "wolf-tooth" as the first cheek tooth. Any injured tooth (broken or cracked from trauma) can develop an infected root, but the third and fourth cheek teeth (the 4th premolar and 1st molar) are predisposed to the development of infected roots without any history of trauma. Also not all of the cheek teeth have roots in the sinus and the horse's age is also a factor as there are more teeth in the sinuses of older horses.

The classic presentation of a horse with a tooth root abscess is one with an incredibly putrid smelling nasal discharge consistently coming from one nostril. The horse is generally bright, alert, responsive, has no fever, usually eats normally, and is normal in every respect with the exception of the stinky nasal discharge. Diagnosis is generally made by taking radiographs of the head. Treatment of a tooth root abscess typically involves removal of the affected tooth and systemic antibiotics and/or flushing of the sinus.

Another problem that could cause a nasal discharge related to a sinus problem includes the growth of a tumor inside one of the sinuses with or without secondary infection.

THE GUTTURAL POUCH

Guttural Pouch Empyema

Guttural pouch empyema (pronounced em-py-ema) is a bacterial infection of the guttural pouch. Affected horses might be free of clinical signs with the exception of a thick, white to yellow nasal discharge, but some are systemically ill. The discharge is most obvious when the horse is eating off of the ground and swallowing. As in us, the opening of the eustachian tube (guttural pouch in the horse) opens up when a horse swallows and with its head down low, the stuff runs right out. Guttural pouch empyema most often is associated with a chronic Streptococcus (Strep) infection which includes one species of Streptococcus that causes strangles (*Strep. equi*). It is important to rule out strangles and the presence of any swollen lymph nodes. If the infection is chronic, concretions of pus called "chondroids"could develop. The presence of chondroids complicates treatment as they must be removed before the infection will clear up. The treatment of guttural pouch empyema typically involves flushing the affected pouch with any one of a variety of flush solutions and the administration of systemic antibiotics.

Guttural Pouch Tympany

Guttural pouch tympany is a disease of foals. The classic clinical appearance of a foal with guttural pouch tympany is that of a chipmunk with its cheeks full. The bulging occurs right behind the jaw as the guttural pouch distends with air and can be tight; the swelling can lead to a partial obstruction of the upper airway and respiratory distress. If a young horse is standing with its head and neck extended in respiratory distress with a large swelling behind its jaw, seek veterinary assistance immediately.

Guttural Pouch Mycosis

Guttural pouch mycosis is a fungal infection of the guttural pouch. It is unknown what exactly is responsible for the development of guttural pouch mycosis. Fungal infections usually result from fungal species that are primary pathogens (organisms that have the ability to cause disease in healthy beings) and affect immune-suppressed individuals or those receiving long term and chronic antibiotic therapy.

The typical site of fungal infection within the guttural pouch, unfortunately, is right on top of the internal carotid artery — the fungal infection often involves the internal carotid artery. For this very fact, any evidence of bleeding from either one or both nostrils should be treated as an emergency and promptly evaluated.

The onset of guttural pouch mycosis can be extremely insidious with, at times, very little warning of a catastrophic hemorrhage. However, there often are several episodes of minor bleeding prior to a more serious bleed as well as a potential history of non-hemorrhagic nasal discharge for variable periods of time prior to the bloody discharge. Horses suffering from guttural pouch mycosis can suddenly hemorrhage to death from a bleeding internal carotid artery.

Again, I must stress that evidence of bleeding from the nostrils should be treated as an emergency and promptly evaluated. It is possible that the bleeding may be associated with other sources of hemorrhage, but if the cause is the guttural pouch, time is of the essence with respect to treatment.

THE LARYNGEAL AREA

Making a diagnosis of laryngeal abnormalities can be extremely difficult as many of the abnormalities can occur only at high speed after the horse has been exercising for some period of time. The development of the high-speed treadmill has lead to great advancements in both the diagnostic capabilities and evaluation of treatments with respect to laryngeal dysfunction. The high-speed treadmill allows the horse to reach near race speeds while allowing for the insertion of the endoscope while exercising. This direct visual evaluation of the laryngeal area while exercising is of great diagnostic use.

DISPLACEMENT OF THE SOFT PALATE

Dorsal displacement of the soft palate is a disease process well known to performance horse owners. The abnormality can be intermittent or persistent and occur only at racing speed and then only after the horse has been exercising for a period of time — facts that can make an accurate diagnosis more difficult or require tread-mill evaluation. If the displacement is persistent, there could be nerve or muscle dysfunction contributing to the persistence of the problem. The majority of horses suffering

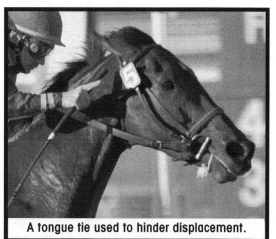

A tongue tie used to hinder displacement.

from displacement do so intermittently. It is a commonly reported cause of upper airway obstruction in the racehorse. Dorsal displacement of the soft palate has been a recognized affliction of horses since 1949, but the specific cause of this problem remains unknown.

Normal placement of the soft palate is essential for unobstructed breathing. The classic history of a horse that displaces the soft palate includes exercise intolerance, generally poor performance, and/or the making of a sudden respiratory noise and simultaneous loss of exercise tolerance — the horse is said to "choke-up" or "swallow the tongue."

The diagnosis is made based on history and an endoscopic examination of the laryngeal area at both rest and while exercising. Many horses can displace their soft palate at rest (and even more so if sedated for the examination), making observation at rest less meaningful. Treadmill evaluation can greatly aid in this diagnosis. It also has been observed that up to 30% of horses suffering from intermittent dorsal displacement of the soft palate have some other throat problem observed during high-speed treadmill examination.

Treatment of a displaced soft palate can involve something as simple as using a "tongue-tie" or a "figure-8" nose band. In addition, if the horse appears generally unfit, an attempt should be made to raise its fitness level. Throat inflammation can be treated using systemic anti-inflammatory drugs and/or the topical application (in the back of the throat) of a variety of anti-inflammatory throat sprays. The tongue tie is an attempt to "pull" the larynx forward and make it harder for the soft palate to displace. Should the tongue tie, nose band, or anti-inflammatory therapy fail as a treatment, there are several surgical options.

The three main options involve trimming part of the soft palate and/or resectioning (surgical cutting) part of the "strap" muscles (the long, thin muscles on the underside of the neck), or changing the shape of the soft palate by injecting certain materials. Both of the palate surgeries can be performed via the endoscope and can involve the use of the laser, and the strap-muscle surgery usually is performed with a local anesthetic. In recent reports, all three of the surgical options indicated an approximate success rate of 60%.

EPIGLOTTIC PROBLEMS

The epiglottis is the triangle-shaped piece of tissue that sits pointing forward at the entrance to the larynx. The epiglottis flips up and covers the opening to the wind-pipe during swallowing and protects against food material entering the respiratory system. Several problems can occur with the epiglottis. There is a generalized inflammation of the epiglottis called epiglottitis (-itis meaning inflammation), the cause of which is unknown. It is hypothesized that other laryngeal abnormalities

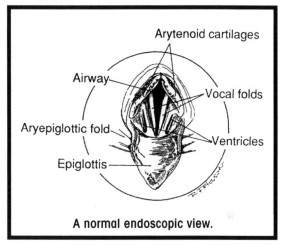

A normal endoscopic view.

could predispose to the inflammation, as well as irritation by allergens, foreign bodies, poor quality roughage (hay), other environmental irritants such as dirt/dust, and/or the stresses involved with performance training. It has been observed that approximately 90% of horses with epiglottic inflammation are racehorses. Clinical signs include ex-

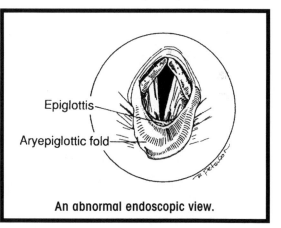

An abnormal endoscopic view.

ercise intolerance, making respiratory noise, coughing, and, occasionally, trouble swallowing or breathing.

Epiglottitis is diagnosed with an endoscope by observing the hallmark signs of inflammation (redness, swelling, ulceration). Treatment involves rest for a minimum of two weeks, with endoscopic re-checks prior to resumption of exercise. Treatment also includes both systemic and topically applied (sprayed up the nose with a catheter) anti-inflammatories. Inflammation of the epiglottis is a serious problem. It has been reported that up to 50% of racehorses affected with epiglottic inflammation developed performance limiting complications.

Epiglottic entrapment is another problem affecting horses. The epiglottis has a firm cartilage inner make-up, so the structure is rather stiff. Epiglottic entrapment is when some of the soft tissue surrounding the epiglottis envelops it and stretches across it like a balloon covering. Clinical signs are similar to those of epiglottic inflammation. The diagnosis is again made by use of the endoscope and observing the classic appearance of the epiglottis entrapped by the soft tissue. Epiglottic entrapment has been observed as a complication in 5% of horses having inflammation of the epiglottis. Treatment of epiglottic entrapment involves cutting away the soft tissue that has entrapped the epiglottis. This procedure often is performed under sedation using a laser via the endoscope.

LARYNGEAL HEMIPLEGIA

Next to the vocal cord area of the larynx are structures called the arytenoids (pronounced a-ryt-e-noids). The arytenoids open and close in a vertical manner and are at the window to the windpipe. During inspiration the arytenoids open wide and allow for maximal air flow through the laryngeal area into the trachea. The arytenoids are moved by a series of small muscles surrounding them under control of the laryngeal nerves. The right laryngeal nerve has a relatively straight shot from the brain to the larynx, but, due to some fluke of nature, the left laryngeal nerve travels from the brain all the way down the neck, flips around one of the major blood vessels near the heart, and travels back up the neck before finally connecting to the muscle responsible for opening the left arytenoid.

This left recurrent laryngeal nerve can degenerate for

unknown reasons and cause the left arytenoid not to open properly. The paralysis of the left arytenoid usually is not complete. Only 10% of horses having this abnormality show complete paralysis and 70% have some degree of asynchronous movement of the arytenoids. The draft breeds appear to be at greater risk for the development of this disease.

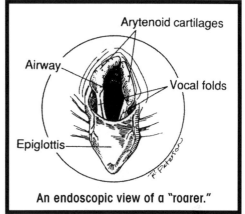

An endoscopic view of a "roarer."

The clinical signs of laryngeal hemiplegia (meaning paralyzed on one side) include respiratory noise on inspiration and/or variable degrees of exercise intolerance. Not all horses experience exercise intolerance, which depends on both the severity of the lesion and a horse's individual performance sport. The noise is a "roaring" type of sound, hence these horses are called roarers. For high-stress endurance horses, the paralysis can affect overall athletic performance and for the less strenuous performers, such as low hunters, the noise produced is considered an "unsoundness" and can result in lower placement in the ribbons.

Diagnosis of left laryngeal hemiplegia is made based on history, clinical signs, resting endoscopic examination, and high-speed treadmill endoscopic examination. The degree of paralysis is graded on a scale of one to four, with four being the worst. If the exercise intolerance is confirmed to result from the airway paralysis or the respiratory noise is unacceptable, surgical intervention is the currently accepted treatment. Surgical correction involves placing a permanent suture into the affected arytenoid and fixing it into the open position.

OTHER INFLAMMATORY CONDITIONS

Other laryngeal abnormalities can predispose to inflammation, as well as irritation by allergens, foreign bodies, poor quality roughage, other inhaled environmental irritants, and/or the stresses involved with performance training. The entire area could be inflamed or just parts of the soft palate, surrounding tissue of the throat, or parts of the larynx itself (the flappers).

The clinical signs associated with throat inflammation include exercise intolerance, making respiratory noise, coughing, and, occasionally, trouble swallowing or breathing. Coughing is one of the more prominent signs, with generalized throat inflammation. Treatment involves rest plus the use of both systemic and topically applied anti-inflammatories.

LYMPH NODES

The tissues of the head are home to many lymph nodes, a series of which surround both guttural pouches and the laryngeal area. Their location next to the larynx and trachea makes them at risk of affecting the respiratory system. One of the more common causes of severe lymph node swelling and abscess formation in the head is strangles, a bacterial infection caused by *Streptococcus equi*.

With strangles, the lymph nodes swell and become large abscesses. It is ideal if an abscess enlarges towards the skin and ruptures/drains outwardly, but sometimes it goes the other way. In severe cases of strangles, the lymph node swelling can become so great that there is enough compression of the laryngeal/upper trachea that airway obstruction occurs. Acute respiratory distress, to the point of requiring a tracheotomy (emergency surgery opening the lower part of the trachea to allow breathing), can be a complication of strangles.

THE LOWER AIRWAY

The lower airway consists of the lungs and the air tubing (bronchi) that supply them. The lungs have some very interesting and unique protective mechanisms that work hard to prevent infection. Obviously the air we breathe is not sterile and contains many contaminants such as dirt, dust, pollen, and chemicals, as well as bacteria, virus particles, and fungal elements. The protection actually starts in the upper airway with filtering, hu-midifying, and warming of the inspired air. The upper respiratory system, trachea, and bronchi are lined with tissue that is covered with a wet, sticky mucus to which air contaminants

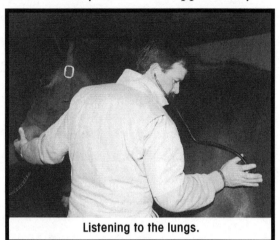

Listening to the lungs.

will stick. Taking the process a step further, the tissue lining the trachea and bronchi has a billion or so cells with ex-tremely small hair-like fibers, or cilia, sticking out in the airway.

The cilia increase the surface area of the filtering surface and play an active role in airway protection. Through a process called mucociliary transport, the debris that is col-lected on the surface of the airways is actually transported away from the lungs. Also called the mucociliary escalator, the small fibers move in a coordinated manner to transport the thin layer of mucus that floats on top of the cilia (and debris stuck to it) out of the lungs and up the trachea where the horse (and we) swallow it. Absolutely disgusting and you don't even know it happens, but it is essential for healthy lung maintenance.

Anything that decreases the effectiveness of the mucocil-iary escalator increases the chances for respiratory disease development. Factors such as cold air, smoke, or chemicals in the air (ammonia fumes from poorly cleaned stalls or bad barn ventilation), and inflammatory conditions of the airways (such as bronchitis and asthma) can decrease the defense mechanism of the mucociliary escalator.

Another way the mucociliary clearance mechanism can be overwhelmed and compromised is forced head posture during transport. If fact, the transportation process can stress the lungs' defense mechanism in several ways. The exhaust fumes from a poorly maintained truck or van can have a negative effect on the mucociliary escalator as can ammonia fumes from a trailer or van with poor drainage. If the ventilation in the trailer or van is bad, it can worsen all of the aforementioned negative factors.

In addition to the mucociliary clearance system, other mechanisms exist to protect the respiratory system against infection. Millions of special cells located deep within lung tissues can kill bacteria and deactivate viruses. Special white blood cells that can engulf and kill invading organisms are plentiful within the lungs and play a vital role in the local immune system. However, the normal function of these cells can be impaired by a number of factors. Many of the aforementioned factors that can decrease the effectiveness of the mucociliary transport also can compromise cellular immunity within the lungs. In addition, the cellular defense mechanisms can be overwhelmed by high concentrations of environmental contaminants. Should infection occur, extra white blood cells from the blood easily can flood the respiratory tissue.

PNEUMONIA

Pneumonia is an umbrella term that simply means "inflammation of the lung." It does not define the actual cause of the inflammation. As we will explore here, the causes of pneumonia are numerous.

Equine Influenza

The equine influenza virus is related to the virus that causes the "flu" in people, although it is different enough that human infection with the equine flu virus does not naturally occur. The flu viruses contain a chemical that damages the mucociliary transport mechanism, allowing for invasion of the immune system. In addition, the damage to the mucociliary transport system can take several days or longer to repair, weakening defense mechanisms and increasing the possibility of secondary bacterial infection. The disease can be extremely contagious, especially in conditions of crowding and poor ventilation — some racetracks have an "outbreak" several times per year.

Influenza most commonly affects 2- and 3-year-olds, with exposure, stresses on the respiratory tract's immune system, and inadequate vaccinations being the predisposing factors. The incubation period is one to three days, and the virus affects the upper respiratory tract to a greater extent than the lungs. Clinical signs, which typically appear three to five days following exposure, include fever, loss of appetite, depression, a clear nasal discharge, and a deep, dry cough. Some horses experience muscle pain (showing a reluctance to walk) and have swollen legs (edema). The course of infection usually runs from two to 10 days if there are no complications; secondary bacterial infection is a common complication of equine influenza. Horses can shed the virus for three to six days after the last signs of illness and should be kept in isolation for that period.

Treatment involves symptomatic care and the use of antibiotics only if a secondary bacterial infection is suspected. One of the greatest risks is that an affected animal will be put back to work too soon. The virus causes a significant amount of tissue damage that requires time to regenerate and heal. Putting a horse back into work too soon raises the likelihood of complications developing. Some horses with severe infections might require one to two months of rest before resuming training — follow your veterinarian's advice regarding the convalescent time.

Young foals can suffer more severely from equine influenza, and developing pneumonia can be fatal. Foals exhibiting signs of respiratory disease should receive veterinary attention as soon as possible.

Regular vaccination can reduce the population at risk significantly and is recommended. Vaccinate younger, athletic horses at four- to six-month intervals. Older horses should receive their boosters at nine- to 12-month intervals.

Equine Herpesvirus (Rhino)

Equine herpesvirus, equine rhino, rhino, and rhinopneumonitis are the same condition. (Rhinopneumonitis means inflammation of the upper airways and lungs.) The known strains of the equine herpesvirus are termed as I, II, III, and IV. It is strains I and IV that are associated with respiratory disease in the horse. Respiratory disease related to the herpes virus most commonly occurs in foals, weanlings, and yearlings. The immunity to herpesvirus infection is short-lived and reinfection is thought to occur. Re-exposure generally results is a milder or subclinical (undetected) infection. In broodmares, abortion could be infection-related. The equine herpesvirus I can cause respiratory disease, abortion, and neurologic disease. Foals can be born suffering from extensive pneumonia (if they are not aborted) and die within 72 hours. Have your veterinarian evaluate immediately any signs of respiratiory distress in a newborn.

The virus does not tolerate being outside of the body for long, so close contact with an infected animal is important for transmission. The clinical signs appear one to three days following infection and cannot be distinguished from influenza symptoms. Treatment is largely supportive and, as with influenza, the convalescent period is extremely important in reducing complications. Vaccination will not prevent the disease, but can reduce its severity. If you have any pregnant mares, they will need to be vaccinated accordingly to prevent abortion. Check with your veterinarian about vaccinating pregnant mares for protection against herpesvirus.

Equine Rhinovirus

There are several equine rhinoviruses that primarily cause mild upper respiratory disease. The equine "rhinovirus" should not be confused with equine "rhino" or "rhinopneu-monitis," which is caused by the equine herpesvirus.

Equine Viral Arteritis

Equine viral arteritis is an inflammation of the blood vessels. The virus can be transmitted by inhalation or sexual contact, can rapidly spread throughout many organs, and can include signs of respiratory distress. The disease also can cause abortion anywhere from 10 to 34 days following exposure.

The incubation period is three to 14 days if the virus is inhaled and six to eight days if passed venereally. Clinical signs include fever, loss of appetite, depression, and potentially a cough, as well as a clear nasal discharge, a bright reddening of the nasal and ocular tissue, and excessive tear production.

Treatment consists mainly of supportive therapy and observation for any secondary bacterial infection. Rest is extremely important, and infected horses should be isolated for three to four weeks past the last observation of clinical signs to prevent transmission. Most horses recover uneventfully, but occasionally young foals die.

Bacterial pneumonia

The air we breathe is not sterile and neither are many parts of the upper respiratory system. There is a constant source of bacteria that could potentially invade the lung. More than a dozen types of bacteria have been implicated in pneumonia in the horse. Most are either common to the horse's environment or are a normal inhabitant of the upper airway or throat area. In most cases of pneumonia, there is some predisposing cause.

Bacterial pneumonia often follows viral pneumonia due to the damage to the normal protective mechanisms and disruption of the local immune system. This situation often occurs when making a horse return to work too soon after a viral respiratory disease. Other stressful events that can lead to the development of bacterial pneumonia include any intense athletic exercise, transportation, poor nutrition (leading to decrease in immune function), and overcrowding. Realistically, many horses experience these factors on a daily basis without problems, but these events all can potentially contribute to respiratory disease.

Clinical signs include fever, depression, inappetence, nasal discharge, coughing, respiratory distress, and the presence of abnormal lung sounds. In more chronic cases, the onset can be slow and vague, marked only by exercise intolerance and weight loss. In some cases the infection can be localized and walled off in the form of an abscess. Sometimes, if the development of the abscess is insidious enough, severe, acute respiratory distress during exercise can be the first sign. Exacerbation of the disease occurs when the lung abscess ruptures or leaks during the stress of exercise.

Diagnosis of bacterial pneumonia often is made based on history, clinical signs, and what the lungs sound like. Ultrasound and radiographs might be necessary to assess completely the extent of the infection. If the clinical signs are severe or antibiotic therapy has been unsuccessful, a transtracheal wash could provide the necessary information to help direct therapy.

Treatment consists of long-term antibiotic therapy, any supportive therapy needed, and rest. The outcome of bacterial pneumonia can be extremely variable and depends on the predisposing causes, duration of infection, amount of lung tissue involved, the specific type(s) of bacteria involved, and the existence of additional complications. Follow your veterinarian's treatment instructions.

Pleuropneumonia

Remember that the pleura is the thin covering of the lung or the thin lining of the thoracic cavity. Pleuritis is an inflammation of the pleura (the space between the body wall and the lung), and pleuropneumonia is both inflammation within the lung and the pleural cavity. In most cases pleuritis is secondary or occurs in conjunction with pneumonia or a ruptured lung abscess that infects the pleural space.

Factors that trigger development of pneumonia are thought to do the same in the development of pleuritis, but specific causes are unknown. Pleuritis in conjunction with pneumonia can greatly complicate and prolong treatment, which can take up to six months. Fatalities can occur. A variety of bacteria can infect the pleural space and the type of individual bacterium can have a great impact on the overall outcome.

Clinical signs of pleuritis/pleuropneumonia include fever, depression, nasal discharge, and inappetance. In addition, pleuritis is an extremely painful disease process — these horses often hurt between the ribs. Some horses will be reluctant to walk, presumably due to the chest pain. In chronic cases, weight loss can be a prominent clinical sign.

A hallmark clinical sign of pleuritis is the build up of fluid within the thoracic cavity. This fluid muffles out the lung sounds in such a way that there is a straight line (a fluid line) of silence parallel to the ground at the junction between fluid and lung. Also, sandpaper-like rubbing sounds, called pleural friction rubs, can be heard with the stethoscope. These abnormalities can be confirmed and further defined with ultrasonography. Pleural cavity fluid is cultured and evaluated microscopically for the presence of bacteria.

There are some forms of thoracic cancer that can produce all of the clinical signs associated with pleuritis. The treatment of pleuritis can be very difficult and relies on long-term antibiotics, supportive therapy, and drainage of the fluid from the thoracic cavity if necessary. Numerous complications can occur on the road to recovery for these horses.

CHRONIC OBSTRUCTIVE PULMONARY DISEASE (COPD)

Chronic Obstructive Pulmonary Disease is otherwise

known as "heaves." Other names for this disease include "chronic pulmonary disease," "chronic airway reactivity," "hyperactive airway disease," "hay sickness," and "broken wind." This disease is characterized by airway obstruction at the level of the bronchi, primarily due to airway constriction similar to asthma in people.

The specific causes of heaves are unknown, but a variety of allergic reactions might be involved. Many clinicians consider heaves to be a hypersensitivity reaction to dusts and molds. The incriminated molds, *Aspergillus* and *Micropolyspora*, are commonly found in poorly cured hay. There are two categories of affected horses. One group appears to react to allergens in the barn and gets better when kept outside and another group (more commonly located in the Southeast) appears to react to allergens in the pasture and get better when kept inside.

Clinical signs include a chronic cough, a cloudy nasal discharge, and difficulty in expiring air. These horses usually take in air relatively well, but have difficulty exhaling. Because COPD is primarily an allergic reaction without the presence of infection, there is generally no fever (unless there is the development of a secondary bacterial infection). Exercise intolerance, weight loss, and not eating are additional clinical signs. Sometimes these horses can get into trouble because they are so focused on breathing they will not (cannot) take the time out from the effort of breathing to eat or drink. Older horses with chronic heaves will have a thickening of the diaphragm noted along the body wall as an indication of the long standing disease process.

Diagnosis is generally based of history and examination of the respiratory system. Sometimes other diagnostic tests, including a transtracheal washing, might be necessary to rule out other secondary problems.

Treatment involves altering the horse's environment. If the horse is affected badly outside, then keep it inside, and vice versa. Wetting the hay (or completely removing hay from the diet) often is necessary as is bedding on non-dusty wood chips or newspaper. If hay is removed from the diet, there are several fermented hay products and other complete feed products on the market. In my experience, the management changes are very important and must occur in addition to the medical management of heaves. Approximately 50% of the horses I have worked on with heaves respond favorably to management changes.

The main focus of medical therapy is to decrease the inflammation associated with the allergic reaction going on within the lungs — the drug of choice for this, as it is for people with asthma, is corticosteroids. During a severe crisis, the main problem is the constricted small airways within the lungs. Use of drugs to dilate the airways can be a great benefit, if not life saving.

Use of systemic therapy requires caution as these drugs can have significant side effects. Corticosteroids suppress the immune system, can predispose to infection, and also have been associated with the development of laminitis. One of the most potent bronchodilator drugs, atropine, can affect gastrointestinal motility and induce colic if used in excess or if the horse is sensitive to it. Many of the other bronchodilator drugs have a narrow range between therapeutic and toxic and have to be administered frequently, making them less useful in the horse. The drug albuterol (common human asthma drug) has been used in the horse but Cornell University's clinical pharmacology laboratory recently determined that albuterol is not absorbed well out of the horse's gastrointestinal system and therefore has no benefit when given orally.

One drug recently approved by the Federal Drug Administration should offer a needed therapy for horses with heaves. The drug clenbuterol (Ventipulmin™) has been used outside the United States for some time now with reported success — the drug can be given orally and is absorbed well from the gastrointestinal tract.

Another method of therapy is the use of inhalers. The inhaler is probably the main line of defense for human asthma sufferers and has, until recently, posed a unique problem for equine use. The development of the Aeromask, by Trudell Medical, Ontario, Canada, has provided an effective way to use inhalant medication in the horse. The system is quite unique and allows for the use of some great human asthma drugs in the form of inhaled steroids, bronchodilators, and other drugs to control allergic inflammation. These drugs have been used successfully with minimal effort to control advanced cases of COPD, but the main drawback is the expense. Many of these drugs cost in excess of $50.00 per inhaler which might only last a few weeks in the horse.

EXERCISE INDUCED PULMONARY HEMORRHAGE (EIPH)

Exercise Induced Pulmonary Hemorrhage is a disease of athletic horses in which hemorrhaging originates in the lungs (the exact location is unknown). Sometimes the bleeding can be subtle enough to be seen only by microscope evaluation of a bronchial aspirate or obvious enough to be observed pouring from the nostrils. The cause of EIPH is unknown.

Other clinical signs include exercise intolerance, respiratory distress, coughing, and excessive swallowing. The diagnosis is generally made by endoscope evaluation within 90 minutes of exercise. The examination of aspirates from the trachea or bronchi looks for the presence of white blood cells

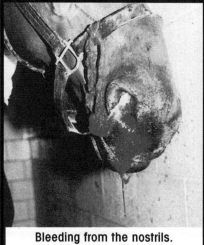

Bleeding from the nostrils.

that have ingested red blood cells as evidence. Treatment of EIPH involves first ruling out the presence of infection, then use of the diuretic drug Lasix (furosemide). Lasix is used primarily in racehorses both as a treatment option and a preventive measure to stop or reduce bleeding. The use of Lasix can be restricted by whichever authority governs the individual equine activities; different states have different regulations.

CHAPTER 10

The Gastrointestinal System

The horse's gastrointestinal system is extremely complex. The small intestine originates from the stomach, which holds approximately two to three gallons of feed material. There is approximately 70 feet of small intestine, which measures about four inches in diameter. At the end of this 70 feet, the small intestine enters a structure called the cecum in the upper right hand side of the flank. The cecum is a large vat that holds approximately 30 gallons and functions to ferment fiber. The cecum is similar to our appendix.

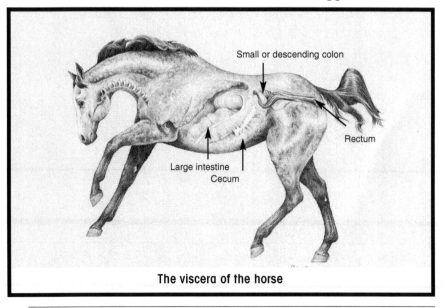

The viscera of the horse

Coming out of the cecum is the right lower large colon. There are approximately 25 feet of large colon. It starts low on the right, coursing forward around the diaphragm, then switching to the left and continuing back to the pelvic area. There, the large colon makes a sharp, narrow turn and continues high on the left, all the way back around the diaphragm again to the upper right side. At that point, the large colon courses to the left side again, becoming the transverse colon, then quickly becoming the 40 feet of small colon. The small

AT A GLANCE

- Gastrointestinal problems are the most common ailment in horses.

- Colic sometimes is tied to changes in a horse's feeding program.

- Flank watching, pawing, and rolling can be signs of abdominal pain.

- Grain overload can lead to laminitis or rupture of the stomach.

- copy

colon, where the fecal balls are made, finally ends at the rectum. The digestion occurs mostly via the fermentation of fiber (hay). Within the colon, there is a normal population of bacteria which ferment the fiber and produce by-products that are absorbed by the intestine and used for nutrition. The fermentation process is very sensitive and can be influenced easily by sudden changes in feed, which can lead to the excess production of gas and the development of colic.

Gastrointestinal tract problems affect the horse more frequently than any other malady. The word "colic" is used as a catch-all term for abdominal distress. In Greek, colic means "affecting the bowels." Fortunately, many bouts of colic are mild and pass without extensive treatment or surgery, but it can be unpredictable and rapidly progress — time can be of the essence in such cases for treatment or surgery to succeed.

Sometimes colic occurs for unknown reasons, but one rather common cause is the alteration of management practices. Sudden changes in feeding habits should be avoided. Many horses which have colicked have had a switch in hay types (usually from a lesser quality grass hay to a high quality alfalfa) or sudden increases in concentrates (grain). The digestion mechanism of horses involves a fermentation process that must maintain a very delicate balance. Anything that alters this balance has the potential to increase gas and/or acid production and can predispose to gastrointestinal problems.

Any changes in feeding habits (including new access to pasture) should be made gradually. When changing types of hay, make sure to get the new hay before the old hay is completely gone and gradually add the new to the old when feeding. It also might be worth the trouble to bring your own feed to shows and avoid adding one more stress to the traveling horse.

Water, in addition to being vital for life, is very important for the health of the gastrointestinal system. Water is actually the most important nutrient. A complete lack of water will kill long before a lack of any other nutrient. Decreased water intake can increase the risk of impaction colic during the cold winter months. It has been shown experimentally that the offering of "room temperature" water during the winter months can as much as double the water intake of some horses. Horses should always have access to fresh, clean water (from clean buckets!) as often as physically possible.

SEVERE ABDOMINAL PAIN

The most obvious signs associated with severe abdominal pain are looking at the belly (flank watching), pawing incessantly, kicking at the belly, and rolling. Other signs include lip curling, inappetence, stretching or posturing to urinate, depression, and flipping or "flagging" of the tail. These latter signs are less specifically associated with abdominal pain and can be caused by other problems.

When a horse demonstrates signs of abdominal pain, consult your veterinarian soon. Many cases of colic are mild and could be related just to excess gas in the intestines, but more serious causes can be difficult for the lay person to distinguish due to the variability of signs, and their intensity, in the individual horse. If the signs reflect a serious problem, time is of the essence.

If the horse is rolling violently, make it rise and keep

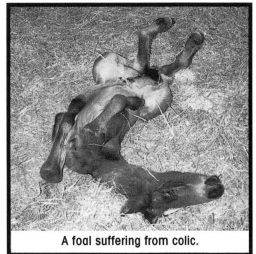

A foal suffering from colic.

it walking to prevent self-injury. Do not allow the horse to eat until veterinary evaluation and recommendation has been made.

GRAIN OVERLOAD (OVEREATING)

The most common situation resulting in grain overload is the horse or pony which escapes from its stall in the middle of the night and hits the jackpot with a 100-pound bag of sweet feed. This also can be a result of feeding excessive quantities of grain or corn to a group of pastured horses — one of them is going to be the alpha horse of the herd and that horse can and will eat more than you intended.

The two major problems associated with grain overload are the development of laminitis and rupture of

Overeating can lead to colic.

the stomach. If you suspect grain overload and the horse is showing signs of colic, get veterinary assistance immediately. Horses cannot vomit, so if there is an indigestion causing a build-up of fluid and/or gas in the stomach, the stomach is at great risk of rupturing if a naso-gastric tube is not passed. Horses with a stomach rupture cannot be saved.

If the horse is not actively painful, prompt veterinary attention still remains important so that appropriate therapy can start. Do not allow the horse to eat while waiting for evaluation.

IMPACTIONS

A common problem which seems to occur more frequently during the winter months is impaction colic. There are several areas where the colon changes in size and if the material within it becomes too dry, the matter can become impacted. Feeding hay probably predisposes to this because the

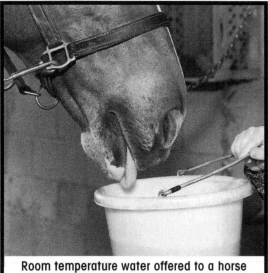

Room temperature water offered to a horse during winter can discourage impaction.

water has been removed (grass is 70% water in the pasture). In the winter months, the horses don't have access to pasture and most seem to have a decrease in water intake as well as a decrease in activity — all of which can predispose to impaction colic. Most of these cases respond to oral administration (via a stomach tube) of a laxative and fluids.

It is important to recognize the early signs. The horses are only mildly painful at first and could be depressed and off feed. The fecal production probably will lessen and the fecal balls will be small, dry, and firm. Offering room temperature water to horses in the wintertime greatly improves water consumption. So the effort to bring warm water to the barn or install water heaters could prove useful in preventing this condition.

CHAPTER 11

The Cardiovascular System

The average 1,000-pound horse has approximately 45 liters (about 11 gallons) of blood that is pumped throughout the body via the veins, arteries, and heart. The main purpose of the cardiovascular system is to pass the blood through the lungs where it picks up oxygen and moves on to all parts of the body to be released and used. The heart is the center of this system and really functions as a very basic pump with a series of valves. As in all species, the horse's heart is comprised of very dense muscle, which is divided into four chambers. Four valves separate the various chambers as well as the entry and exit points.

The average-sized horse has a heart approximately the size of a volleyball. The heart is divided into the right heart and the left heart with two chambers on each side: one on top and one on the bottom. The top chambers are called the atria and the lower chambers are called the ventricles. Blood that is poor in oxygen travels on the right side of the heart. Oxygen-poor blood enters the heart from both the front and hind directions relative to the heart. Oxygen-rich blood has gone through the lungs and travels on the left side of the heart. The large cranial (front) vena cava and caudal (hind) vena cava are the blood vessels to which all of the body's oxygen-poor blood eventually flows. So, the oxygen-poor blood enters the right atrium from the cranial and caudal vena cava. At the same time that the right atrium is filling with poorly oxygenated blood returning from the body, the left atrium is filling with oxygen-rich blood coming from the lungs.

The contraction cycle of the heart has two major cycles: 1) contraction of the atria, which gets an extra amount of blood into the ventricles, and 2) contraction of the ventricles, which moves blood out of the heart and into the lungs or the body. As the atria contract, the blood

AT A GLANCE

• The horse's heart is divided into four chambers.

• The SA-node controls heart rate.

• Arrythmias and valve abnormalities are the two major heart problems.

• Poor performance or exercise intolerance sometimes is a sign of a heart problem.

• A stethoscope can be used to detect abnormalities.

is forced into the ventricles (which have passively filled with blood), pushing in just a little more blood into the larger chambers of the heart. The ventricles then contract with the pressure created, causing the main valves (the tricuspid on the right and the mitral on the left) to slam closed between the atria and the ventricles, thus causing the "lub" of the "lub-dub" sound heard when listening to the heart with a stethoscope. The poorly oxygenated blood in the right ventricle is moved into the lungs where it will pick up oxygen. Well-oxygenated blood in the left ventricle is moved into the main artery of the body — the aorta — where it supplies the whole body. Just after the ventricles finish their contraction and the blood has moved out of the heart, the valves on the heart's exit, the pulmonic on the right and the aortic on the left, slam shut, preventing the blood from back flowing into the heart. This causes the "dub" sound of the "lub-dub." Then, the whole cycle starts over again and continues about 40 times a minute for the life of the horse.

There are a number of factors controlling the rate at which the heart beats. The nervous system has some influence, but the day-to-day normal heart rate is controlled by the heart itself. The heart has its own little nervous system and a timer

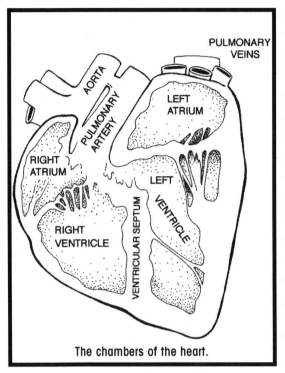

PULMONARY VEINS

AORTA

PULMONARY ARTERY

LEFT ATRIUM

RIGHT ATRIUM

LEFT

VENTRICLE

RIGHT VENTRICLE

VENTRICULAR SEPTUM

The chambers of the heart.

called the "SA-node." The excitation and contraction of the heart, like that of all muscles, is electrical in nature and highly dependent on the movement of calcium and sodium particles that cause the electrical signal. The SA-node lives in the left atrium. The path of the electrical conduit of the heart goes from the SA-node to another center called the "AV-node" which lives between the atria and the ventricles. As the SA-node fires, it causes the muscle tissue of the atria to contract and sends a direct signal with perfect timing to the AV-node which then causes the muscle tissue of the ventricles to contract at just the right time. It is a complicated, beautiful, and mind-boggling system that works day in, day out to move blood around the body.

PROBLEMS WITH THE HEART

Arrythmias

The two major things that can go wrong with the heart are problems with the rhythm of the heart beat and development of valve abnormalities. As mentioned before, the coordination and rhythm of contraction is controlled by a complicated and somewhat delicate balance of both inward and outward influences. The development of an abnormal rhythm is called an arrhythmia. The common arrhythmias of the horse are an increased heart rate (tachycardia), a decreased heart rate (bradycardia), and an abnormal contraction of the atria called "atrial" fibrillation. There are other more complicated arrhythmias that horses occasionally share with people but will not be discussed here.

Tachycardia, or increased heart rate, can be caused by a number of problems: pain, blood loss, fright, toxins or poisons, chemical or electrolyte imbalances within the body, and/or dehydration to name a few. The abnormal elevation of the heart rate (normal is 28 to 44 beats per minute) is a vague clinical sign and can be caused by a primary heart problem or something secondary. A horse with an elevated heart rate should have a thorough physical examination by a veterinarian to ascertain the cause.

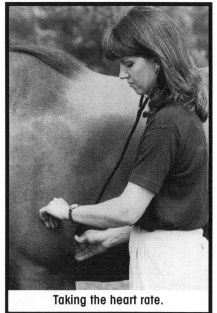

Taking the heart rate.

Bradycardia, or decreased heart rate, is less common and again can be caused by a variety of problems — both primary heart problem or secondary to another problem. One cause that is extremely important to recognize is hypoglycemia, or low blood sugar, in a foal. The foal (from birth throughout the first month of life) has a normal heart rate that is considerably higher than an adult horse — the normal heart rate for a foal of this age can range from 70 to 100 beats per minute. If a young foal is weak, depressed, and has a low heart rate, it can be a clinical sign of hypoglycemia. It is important to recognize this and treat it as a veterinary emergency as death can soon follow.

Atrial fibrillation is an abnormality in which the atria do not contract in a coordinated fashion and just flutter on top of the ventricles. This abnormality usually does not affect the contraction of the ventricles and therefore only causes a small decrease in overall blood output from the heart; the atria only account for 25% to 30% of the blood moved by the heart. The condition generally presents as a poor performance problem and sometimes includes a history of exercise-induced pulmonary hemorrhage (the horse may have been a bleeder). The relationship between the two is unknown. The condition is diagnosed based on the presence of an "irregularly-irregular" heart rhythm and confirmed with a characteristic ECG (electrocardiogram) pattern. Atrial fibrillation can be treated with drugs (generally successfully).

Valve Abnormalities

The presence of a heart murmur is typically an indication of a valve abnormality. The two main heart sounds are caused by the valves slamming shut under back pressure of the blood as it is pumped into and out of the heart. These sounds, as mentioned before, are heard as the "lub-dub" sound with "lub" being the closure of the tricuspid and mitral valves and the "dub" being caused by the closure of the pulmonic and aortic valves. Murmurs are caused by turbulent blood flow resulting from either an obstruction of blood as it is being pumped out of the heart or the leakage of blood back into the heart caused by a "leaky" valve. The sound of the murmur is caused by the turbulent blood flow.

The contraction cycle of the heart also is defined by the time that the heart is passively filling with blood or the time that the heart is contracting and pumping blood. The passive filling time is called diastole and the contraction/pumping time is called systole. The common blood pressure measurements diastolic and systolic refer to the blood pressure during each of these cycles of the heart. These cycles can be identified by listening to the heart and feeling the pulse at the same time. Diastole is the time when there is no bound to the pulse and the heart is relaxed and filling with blood. Systole is when the bound of the pulse can be detected and the heart is contracting and causing the pulse wave.

Heart murmurs are characterized by the location (over which valve they are loudest), the character of the sound they make, and whether they occur during diastole, systole, or both. They are graded based on loudness on a scale of one to five or one to six.

The most common heart murmur that horses get is an aortic insufficiency murmur which is caused by a leaky aortic valve. Because the murmur is caused by a leakage of blood back into the heart from the aorta, it occurs during diastole - just after the heart relaxes, the blood back flows into it, causing turbulence and thus the murmur. The murmur is obviously loudest over the aorta and is typically loud and very "musical" in sound quality. To contrast this, a much less common murmur is an aortic "stenotic" murmur. Stenosis means "narrowed." If the aorta is narrowed where it attaches to the heart there will be turbulence as the blood is pumped through the narrowed area — in this case the murmur would be during systole.

The aortic insufficiency murmur is caused by the development of an irregular edge to the aortic valve. The murmur is thought to be an "old age" change and generally does not cause a physical problem. The murmur can be disturbing because this type can be very loud, but if the murmur is solely

Certain heart problems can cause a horse to collapse or die.

aortic insufficiency there is little overall effect on the horse's health. The heart should be thoroughly evaluated to ensure that there are no other problems.

A more serious murmur in horses is a mitral insufficiency murmur. The mitral valve is the valve between the left atria and left ventricle and slams closed when the left ventricle contracts, moving oxygenated blood out the aorta and to the body. The murmur is during systole and causes a more serious problem because it decreases the amount of oxygenated blood getting pumped out of the heart. As the left ventricle contracts, the valve slams shut but leaks, letting some of the blood flow back into the left atria — the turbulence of the blood jetting past the valve causes the murmur. This murmur can be caused by the rupture of some of the support structures of the valve. The mitral valve has three leaflets with cord-like tissue that attach the free edge of the valve to the heart muscle in the ventricle (the valve is almost like a parachute with the cords). If the cord tissue ruptures, the valve will flap backwards into the atria and become leaky.

The signs of acute mitral valve rupture are extreme exercise intolerance (many pull up while working and are extremely prostrate), collapsing, tremors, high heart rate, rapid breathing, blue gums, colic, and/or death. A more chronic mitral valve murmur might have no clinical signs or just exercise intolerance. The aortic insufficiency and mitral insufficiency murmurs are two of the relatively common heart murmurs that horses develop, but there are others which are caused by turbulence of blood flow within the heart for a variety of reasons.

The diagnosis of heart murmurs obviously is based on hearing them with the stethoscope. A common clinical sign, if the murmur is causing a problem, is exercise intolerance. Once a murmur is detected, the most accurate and sensitive way to evaluate the heart and the murmur's extent is by using diagnostic ultrasound. The use of ultrasound will allow the direct imaging of the heart — the chamber size, the muscle thickness, the valve structures — and a number of other details that will aid in determining the significance of a heart murmur.

CHAPTER 12

The Ocular System

We all have worked with a horse which just completely freaked out over some really stupid thing on the ground or in the barn that has been there for years. What is it about today that caused the tarp on the ground or spray bottle on the ledge of a stall to trigger the release of every inner demon in your horse's mind? Could it be the beginning of a vision problem? Most likely not, but it never hurts to rule it out.

Theories and controversy regarding exactly how a horse visually perceives its world have existed for more than a century. The main questions asked and remaining ones to be answered definitively are: 1) Does the horse bring a visual image into focus using the "focusing" system of the lens, as people do, or via movement of the head? 2) Does a horse see in color? and 3) Do horses suffer from visual defects, similar to people, such as near-sightedness (myopia) or far-sightedness (hyperopia) that might affect performance?

Whatever the answers to these questions, normal vision is extremely important to the horse's daily existence. As stated by the late James Law, professor of veterinary science, Cornell University, in a 1923 edition of a U.S. Dept. of Agriculture Special Report of Diseases of the Horse: "We can scarcely overestimate the value of sound eyes in the horse, and hence all the diseases and injuries which seriously interfere with vision are matters of extreme gravity and apprehension…as a mere matter of beauty, a sound, full, clear, intelligent eye is something which must always add a high value to our equine friends and servants."

> ## AT A GLANCE
>
> • How a horse sees is not entirely understood.
>
> • A horse might focus by raising or lowering its head.
>
> • Squinting, tearing, and sensitivity to light indicate eye pain.
>
> • Uveitis is the leading cause of equine blindness.

The essence of the visual system is to collect light and focus it onto the retina in the back of the eye, where the image then is transmitted to the brain via the nervous system. To the point where the light, and hence the image, is focused on the retina, the eye functions very much like a camera lens. In people and domestic animals the lens (the soft structure that sits behind the pupil) can have its shape changed by small muscles. This change in shape brings an image into focus on the retina. If the light image is not in focus, then the image perceived by the brain is not in focus — time for glasses or contacts!

The controversy of the "ramped retina" started in 1930. It is known that, relative to other species, the horse's lens does not have a great ability to change shape and therefore might not be capable of being the sole mechanism of focusing light on the retina. It was proposed in 1930, 1942, and 1960 by independent researchers that the retina and hence the back of the equine eye is not perfectly round, but in fact sloped or "ramped." In short, this means that the horse might be able to "find" a location on the retina where the light is in focus by raising or lowering its head. A 1975 study failed to support the previous findings, but a 1977 study supported the idea of the horse having to move its head or eye, or both, for optimal visual acuity. It is generally believed that the horse must elevate its head to "focus" on objects close to it and conversely lower its head to focus on objects far away.

ANATOMY OF THE EYE

Before getting into the eye examination, it is important to understand the anatomy of the eye. The outer surface of the eye is called the cornea. The cornea is very thin (approximately a half-millimeter) and should be clear. Behind the

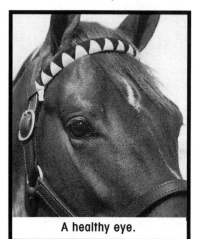

A healthy eye.

cornea is the space known as the anterior (front) chamber. This is the space that exists between the inner surface of the cornea and surface of the iris and lens and is filled with fluid called the aqueous humor. The iris is typically brown tissue encircling the black pupil. This is the tissue that constricts or dilates the pupil depending on the light intensity. The lens is a soft structure that sits in the pupil. It is normally clear. The blackness of the pupil is caused by the dark inner eye. From the posterior (back) surface of the lens comes a clear, jelly-like substance called the vitreous, then the retina on the posterior part of the eye. The retina is a thin, translucent layer that transmits light information to the brain via the optic nerve that enters the back of the eye. This can be seen in the back of the eye as a small white dot (the optic disk).

THE EYE EXAM

At present, vision testing in horses is not an exact science. The main goal of the ophthalmic examination is to identify abnormalities of the eye and speculate on how they could affect vision based on known structure and function of the eye. Obviously, if there is a large, dense scar on the cornea from a prior corneal infection or a very dense cataract (opacity of the lens), vision will be affected. The difficulty is trying to ascertain to what degree smaller lesions affect total vision.

The examination starts with historical information. Is the horse head-shy in the absence of behavior modification techniques, such as getting smacked in the muzzle for biting frequently? Does the horse have a "sidedness" to the head-shyness, i.e., only when someone or something is on a particular side of the horse? Does the horse have similar behavior when turned out in pasture, free in the stall, or just when being worked? Has there ever been any head trauma — hit its head on the trailer? kicked in the head? hit its head in the starting gate? flipped over on the cross-ties?

The next step is to stand back and look at the horse. Is there anything abnormal about the appearance of the eyes? Are they symmetrical? Does the horse have any scars or fresh wounds only on one side of the head that might indicate frequently bumping into things on that side? If there are positive historical or general examination findings, this raises suspicion for a visual deficit.

The first test performed to determine if the horse can see is called the "menace." This test is just that. A menacing gesture is made toward the horse's eye with the hand to see if the horse will blink. This must be done carefully so that 1) the other eye cannot see the movement as both eyelids will blink, and 2) the motion of the hand does not touch the lashes or create a strong enough current of air to be felt, both of which will make the horse blink. Obviously if the horse is totally blind or has significant visual impairment, it will not blink, but if there is a partial "blind-spot," it cannot be well assessed in this manner.

The two common instruments used in assessing the horse's eye are a penlight or other strong focal light source and an ophthalmoscope. The eye is evaluated using a systematic approach looking for corneal scars, abnormalities in the anterior chamber, iris, or lens.

Corneal scars result from some prior corneal infection or trauma. Depending on the cause, they can vary in size from pin head to the majority of the cornea. If they are small it is likely that they don't affect vision significantly and, as one would assume, the larger they are the greater the chance of having a negative effect on vision.

On rare occasion, cysts on the iris can be observed hanging down over the pupil like a small punching bag. If large

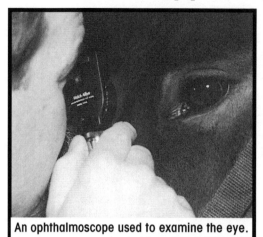

An ophthalmoscope used to examine the eye.

enough, these iris cysts can obstruct the pupil and actually move in the aqueous humor which could create a moving "shadow" or visual deficit to which the horse might react. Some horses, after suffering from inflammation in the anterior chamber (infection, uveitis), the iris can lose function from an adhesion to the surface of the lens. These horses cannot dilate their pupil in low light environments or the adhesion can be significant enough to obstruct the pupil.

Cataracts are rare in adult horses and usually secondary to a prior ocular trauma or chronic uveitis, but can obstruct the light flow through the eye and affect vision. The larger and more dense the cataract, the greater chance it will affect vision.

The ophthalmoscope evaluates the fundus or back of the eye at 15 times magnification. The health of the optic nerve can be evaluated and the remainder of the fundus evaluated for scars. Eyes that have suffered from uveitis or severe ocular inflammation from other causes can develop scar tissue as well as dysfunctional areas of the retina. These scarred areas can be related to "blind spots" in vision and the larger the scars the greater the chance of a significant effect on vision. A more unusual finding in the fundus is a "vitreal floater." Sometimes after serious inflammation in the back of the eye, the vitreous humor becomes more liquid and small collections of inflammatory debris actually can "float" around. It has been hypothesized that this "debris," if large enough, could disrupt the visual field when a horse moves its head, thus causing it to spook. However, the true relationship between the floater and the behavior is unknown.

What if the eye inspects normally but is blind? This is where history can be helpful. In some cases of head trauma the eye is not overtly damaged, but the optic nerve might have been damaged. It can take several weeks or longer for the damage to become apparent. It is often said that this is a disease in which the patient sees nothing and the doctor sees nothing.

COULD A HORSE NEED GLASSES?

There was a report from the American Museum of Natural History in 1961 indicating that a portion of domesticated horses are near-sighted (myopic). Myopia is when light and the image comes into focus in front of the central part of the retina. The image the brain perceives as determined by the retina is blurred. But if the horse does have a "ramped retina," it might be able to raise or lower its head until the image is in focus. This, of course, is speculation and what image is truly perceived by the horse's brain as it gazes out on the horizon of a summer pasture most likely will remain a mystery to humans for eternity.

PERIODIC OPHTHALMIA

Periodic ophthalmia, otherwise known as recurrent uveitis, uveitis, or moon blindness, can be a devastating disease about which we know little. The hypothetical causes have been re-searched sporadically over the years, but we really aren't much closer to understanding this inflammatory ocular disease. The term "moon blindness" comes from the ancient belief that the disease was associated with the changes of the lunar cycles. The "recurrent" or "periodic" part of the disease is because of the propensity of this disease to recur in a rather unpredictable manner. The medically descriptive name for this disease is uveitis (pronounced U-V-itis) and I will call it that for the rest of this chapter. The uvea is an anatomical name for certain parts of the interior eye and, of course "itis" means inflammation — so uveitis is an inflammation of the uvea. The uvea includes most of the interior parts of the eye that have a large blood supply. This is especially true for the iris or colored part of the eye surrounding the pupil.

WHO SUFFERS FROM UVEITIS?

All species of animals, including humans, can suffer from some form of uveitis, but the horse has been plagued with the recurrent form of this disease for some time. If fact, this disease was recorded by veterinarians attending horses of Alexander the Great. The disease is reported to have a world-

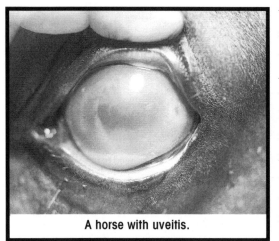

A horse with uveitis.

wide distribution, but it appears to be more common in North America than in Australia, the United Kingdom, or South Africa. Uveitis probably suffers from more folklore, ignorance, misconception, and anecdotal causes, cures, and treatments than any other human or veterinary disease yet discovered. Unfortunately, the bottom line is that we really don't know very much about recurrent uveitis. Although there are many "predisposing" factors scattered about in the lay literature as well as specific horse predispositions, there are no age, sex, breed, moon cycle, or any other proven predisposing factors. It has been reported that up to 12% of a given population of horses in some areas of the eastern United States can suffer from uveitis. The specific proven causes and those under investigation will be discussed in the next section of this chapter.

THE SUSPECTED CAUSES

Uveitis can result from anything that causes inflammation within the eye and does not necessarily have to be associated with recurrent uveitis. Trauma to the eye can induce uveitis. Just blunt trauma, e.g., a pop in the eye with a polo ball, can create inflammation and propagate uveitis. If the trauma involves a wound of any sort to the eye, then uveitis can be caused by infection. If a corneal ulcer caused by bacteria, fungi, or yeast becomes severe enough and starts to involve the deeper layer of the cornea it can induce uveitis. Sometimes these corneal infections actually can rupture into the anterior chamber and cause a very severe uveitis. In addition, severe systemic infection (most typically neonatal septicemia) can have a uveitis component. The presence of uveitis in a neonate can indicate a systemic disease.

With respect to recurrent uveitis or periodic opthalmia, research shows that currently suspected causes include infection with the bacteria *Leptospira* and *Streptococcus equi* (the cause of strangles) and the parasite *Onchocerca cervicali*. The most commonly held explanation is that inflammation of the uvea is caused by a delayed hypersensitivity reaction or is an autoimmune-mediated phenomenon. A delayed hypersensitivity reaction is one of the four classic immune responses to a foreign substance in our body. Essentially there is an autoimmune-mediated reaction developing after exposure to a foreign substance. Some of the immune cells have a memory of the foreign substance and are suspected to persist on the uveal tissue. Then, when the horse (and subsequently the immune cells) are exposed to the same foreign substance sometime in the future, the reaction stimulates inflammation.

The autoimmune phenomenon occurs when the immune system, for whatever reason, stops recognizing a part of the body as part of the family and starts to reject it. It could be possible that after infection with one of the suspected causes of recurrent uveitis, immunoproteins (antibodies) are produced that might target the uveal tissue. If the protein structure of part of the infectious agent is similar to the protein structure of part of the uveal tissue, this situation might occur. A classic example of this in people is Rheumatic fever in which the heart valves are attacked by the immune system after infection with the bacteria that causes strep throat.

CLINICAL SIGNS

Clinical signs for this disease can be broken up into those observed during an acute flare-up of the disease and those that indicate the disease has occurred in the past. The primary sign of uveitis is pain as manifested by squinting, tearing, and an increased sensitivity to light. Other observed signs are a very constricted pupil (even in a dark stall), cloudiness within the eye (will be difficult to see the iris and pupil with a distinct haze present), and the presence of solid material (protein) attached to the iris. As the inflammation occurs within the eye, irritating chemicals are produced and released into the fluid in the anterior chamber (the space filled with a clear fluid between the inside of the cornea and the iris). In addition to the release of inflammatory chemicals, white blood cells and protein leak from the inflamed blood vessels into the anterior chamber fluid, creating the haze within the anterior chamber. In severe cases of uveitis, the white blood cells will settle and collect in the floor of the anterior chamber. One of the proteins that leaks into the anterior chamber is called fibrin. Fibrin is a light, fluffy, cotton candy-like substance that is a precursor to a dense, connective tissue scar. If the fibrin production in the eye is heavy and goes without treatment, this stuff actually can cause a significant amount of scarring within the eye. Matured fibrin can glue the iris to the lens, thus preventing it from opening in lower light situations or cover the lens and greatly affect vision. If left untreated, the inflammation can have a devastating impact on vision.

The signs of prior uveitis can be more subtle and require extensive examination of both the outer and inner areas of the eye. This examination is an important part of the pre-purchase examination due to the recurrent nature of uveitis. Unfortunately, it is impossible for your veterinarian to predict if the uveitis will recur. The disease might never happen again or could recur next week and there really is no way to predict. All your veterinarian can do is attempt to determine how the damage affects vision and document the extent of the lesions. The most subtle signs is a darkening of the iris to a dark chocolate color without obvious scarring of the iris itself. In advanced cases it can appear moth-eaten and scarred. The edge of the iris may be irregular and roughened. (Remember, the little punching bag-like gizmos — nigra bodies — on the iris are normal and must be differentiated from abnormal irregularities.)

Also the surface of the lens (within the pupil area) might have a piece of brown iris stuck to it (or the iris itself) or other scar tissue from the previous inflammation. Sometimes there are white strands of scar tissue darting about inside the anterior chamber.

The most crucial part of the examination with respect to pre-purchase is deep inside the eye. It is possible not to have any of the other tell-tale signs and have significant scarring in the back of the eye. The lesions caused by uveitis in the back of the eye (where the light sensing retina is) are reflective scars surrounding the optic disk (optic nerve as it enters the eye). These lesions are referred to as "butterfly" lesions as they often appear in the shape of a butterfly. The scarring in the back of the eye, depending on the degree of it, can cause a visual deficit or blind spot.

In more chronic cases of uveitis, the iris can become very scarred and light in color; the border of the iris is very irregular and glued down to the lens; the lens opacified by the presence of a cataract; the eye abnormally large and firm or small and soft; and vision could be severely impaired. Also in advanced cases the cornea might not be healthy and could have an ulcer. In all cases one or both eyes could be affected.

TREATMENT

Before initiating treatment for uveitis, it is imperative that a veterinarian make the diagnosis and evaluate the cornea for the presence of a corneal ulcer. The two main drugs used in the treatment of uveitis are atropine and corticosteroids. The atropine serves several important purposes. Atropine works by paralyzing some of the muscles of the iris, thus stopping the painful spasm and allowing the pupil to dilate. Dilation is very important to reduce the chances that the iris will become scarred to the lens. Sometimes if the atropine alone does not dilate the pupil, another drug will be used that actively dilates the pupil.

Corticosteroids are potent anti-inflammatory drugs that are typically necessary to reduce the inflammation of a uveitic eye. Corticosteroids are not a risk-free treatment. Due to their potent immune-suppressing abilities, the corticosteroids, if used on an eye in the presence of a corneal ulcer, can predispose to a fungal eye infection. Approximately 65% of horses which develop fungal eye disease have been treated with a topical corticosteroid. Despite this risk, the corticosteroids are necessary to control the inflammation associated with uveitis.

In addition to these two main treatments for uveitis, topical antibiotics, topical antifungal, and topical non-steroidal anti-inflammatory are used. Systemic pain medication often is necessary, too. There also is a rather neat (but unfortunately expensive) treatment used if the fibrin content in the anterior chamber is severe. The greater the fibrin content in the anterior chamber the greater the chance of permanent scarring and visual deficit. A drug called TPA (tissue plasminogen activator), which is used as a clot buster in human heart attack and stroke patients, can be injected directly into the eye to dissolve the fibrin.

Another treatment that might need consideration is removal of a severely infected eye. This can be a very difficult decision to make, but sometimes represents the best option for the horse. A chronic uveitis eye can be painful and require substantial treatment to achieve even marginal comfort with no vision remaining. At this time, the animal might be blind in that particular eye and suffer from chronic pain. The best way to remove the pain might be to remove the eye.

Hopefully sometime in the near future there will be a research breakthrough in the prevention or treatment of uveitis, but until then uveitis will remain the leading cause of blindness in horses.

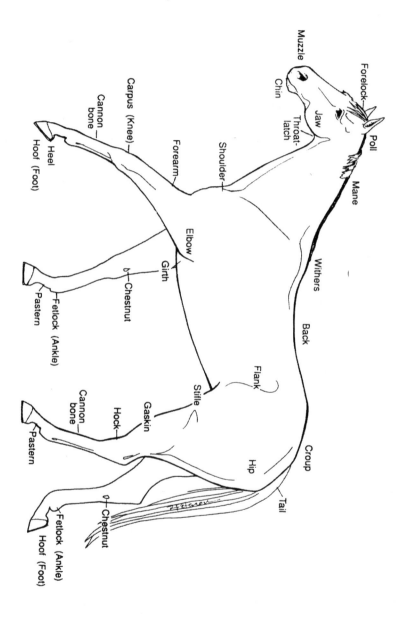

Parts of the horse

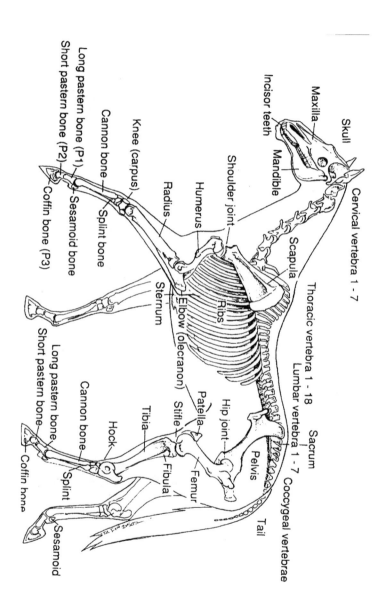

Skeletal system

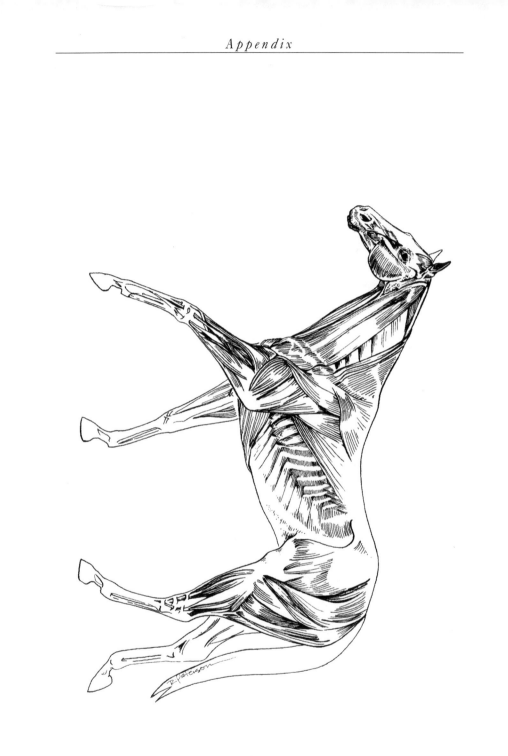

Muscular system

GENERAL HORSE FACTS

Bones: A horse has approximately 205 bones.

Teeth: There are 24 deciduous (baby) teeth and 40 or 42 permanent (adult) teeth. The "canine" teeth are the ones between the incisors and the first check tooth (where the bit goes) and are usually present only in male horses.

Blood: There is approximately 10 gallons of circulating blood in a 1,000-pound horse.

Hoof growth: The hoof grows an average of 1 centimeter per month.

Body temperature: The normal body temperature of the horse is 100° F (38° C) +/- 1° F.

Heart rate: The normal heart rate ranges from 24 to 40 beats per minute.

Respiratory rate: The normal respiratory rate ranges from 10 to 16 breaths per minute.

Reproduction: The mare cycles based on season; she comes into heat every three weeks during spring and early summer.

Gestation length: The average gestation length is 341 days, ranging from 315 to 365 days.

Aging of horses by the teeth

The age of horses can be determined very accurately by the teeth up to age 10, after which it involves some guesswork. By one year of age, all three baby incisor teeth are erupted and the first and second ones are in wear. By two, the first and second baby incisor teeth are level. At 2½ years the first permanent incisor erupts. At 3½, the second permanent incisor erupts, and at 4½ years, the third permanent incisor erupts. By age five, all the permanent incisors are in wear and most male horses have erupted canine teeth. The next step in determining age involves observing the disappearance of the "cup" in the lower incisor teeth. The cup is the indentation in the center of the tooth's chewing surface. The cup wears away in the first, second, and third incisor at six, seven, and eight years of age, respectively.

Acupuncture — The Chinese art of placing needles into certain points on the body to re-establish proper energy within the body.

Arrhythmia — An irregular rhythm to the heart beat.

Atria — Two of the four chambers of the heart.

Atrial fibrillation — A common abnormal heart rhythm occurring in horses.

Bleeder — A horse suffering from exercised-induced pulmonary hemorrhage (EIPH).

Blind spavin (occult spavin) — A disease that originates in the hock joint and causes typical spavin lameness but shows no palpable or radiological changes. Least common of the spavins.

Blood spavin — No true definition. It usually applies only to an enlarged vein crossing a bog spavin.

Bog spavin — A chronic inflammation of the lining of the tibio-tarsal joint characterized by distension of the joint capsule.

Bone spavin — Spavin is usually described as a periostitis or osteitis (inflammation of the bone and its covering) involving the bones of the hock joint. 1) Jack spavin — a bone spavin of large proportions. 2) High spavin — a bone spavin located higher on the hock joint than ordinary bone spavin.

Bowed tendon — Damage to the tendon causing inflammation and enlargement of the tendon.

Bruised sole — A term applied to bruises on the front aspect of the foot other than those found at the seat of corn. The cause is usually direct injury from stones, irregular ground, other trauma, or bad shoeing.

Bucked shins — A periostitis (inflammation of the covering of the bone) of the anterior surface of the large metacarpal or metatarsal bone. The condition is most often seen in the forelegs of young Thoroughbreds in training and racing.

Canker — A chronic over-growth of the horn-producing tissues of the foot, involving the frog, the sole and, at times, the wall.

It is most often found in hind feet and primarily a disease of the heavy draft horse.

Caps — Sometimes with premolar teeth, the root of the temporary tooth can be absorbed, but the crown persists as a covering or "cap" to the erupting permanent tooth; these caps are readily removed with forceps, if they have not separated spontaneously.

Cecum — A part of the large intestine that is analogous to our appendix.

Colic — Generic term for a problem affecting the gastrointestinal system.

Contracted heels — A condition most commonly seen affecting the quarters and heels of the front feet of light-boned horses. It might be caused by improper shoeing that draws in the quarters and does not allow frog pressure.

COPD — Chronic obstructive pulmonary disease or heaves, an allergic airway disease.

Corns — Bruising of the sole, in the angle between the wall and the bar, usually in the inner quarter and most commonly in the forefeet.

Coronary band — The area at the junction between the hoof wall and the skin.

Cribbing — The horse habitually sets its upper incisor teeth on a firm object such as a manger, and sucks in and swallows air, usually with a characteristic grunting sound.

Curb — A thickening or "bowing" of the plantar tarsal ligament (the ligament is the one that slopes down from the point of the hock) due to a strain.

Ear tooth (ectopic tooth, dentigerous tooth, temporal odontoma) — Commonly located in the mastoid process of the petrous temporal bone (the bone up by the ear) and is recognized by the presence of a discharging sinus along the edge of the ear.

Guttural pouch — A special structure in the head that can be involved in several disease processes.

Guttural pouch mycosis — Fungal infection of the guttural pouch.

Heart murmur — A noise created by turbulent blood flow within the heart usually due to a leaky heart valve.

Hyaluronic acid — A natural substance in synovial fluid that is considered to be a joint lubricant.

Inflammation — The tissue response to injury, creating the hallmark signs of redness, heat, pain, swelling, and reduced function.

Keratitis — Inflammation of the cornea of the eye.

Keratoma — An inflammatory non-cancerous growth of horn on the inner surface of the wall, usually at the toe.

Laminitis (founder) — Inflammation of the tissues that connect the hoof wall and the coffin bone.

Ligaments — The soft tissue structure that connects bone to bone.

Nail bind (gathered nail) — Puncture wound of the foot.

Osslets (osselets) — An inflammation of the bone covering (periosteum) on the lower front epiphyseal surface of the large metacarpal bone (cannon bone) and the associated capsule of the fetlock joint.

Parrot mouth — An overbite, caused by the upper jaw overhanging the lower and resulting in imperfect apposition of the teeth of the upper and lower incisors.

Periodic ophthalmia — Moon blindness or uveitis.

Pleuritis — Inflammation of the thoracic cavity.

Pleuropneumonia — Inflammation of the thoracic cavity.

Pneumonia — Inflammation in the lungs.

Popped knee (carpitis, sore knee) — An acute or chronic inflammation of the joint capsule (soft tissue surrounding the joint) and associated structures of the carpus.

Poultice — A topical product designed to increase blood flow into inflamed tissue, usually used on the legs.

Rhabdomyolysis (tying up) — A muscle disorder leading to muscle swelling, inflammation, and pain.

Rhinitis — Inflammation of the nasal passages.

Rhinopneumonitis — Inflammation of the lungs, caused by

the equine herpesvirus.

Ringbone — A periostitis or osteoarthritis leading to bone growth involving the first or second phalanx.

Roaring — The making of respiratory noise related to laryngeal hemiplegia.

Sand crack (toe crack, quarter crack) — Any break in the continuity of the hoof wall that begins at the coronet and runs parallel to the horn tubules. Quarter crack is most often seen in racehorses.

Saw mouth (prominent chin, bulldog jaw) — The opposite of parrot mouth; it is less common in horses. If a foal is badly affected, sucking is impossible.

Sharp teeth — The most common equine dental "disease," characterized by the presence of sharp edges or points on the cheek teeth (outside of the top, inside of the bottom).

Shear mouth — This can be considered an extreme form of sharp teeth with an exaggerated obliquity of the molar tables. It usually is seen in old horses and may involve two or more opposing teeth but can occur in all arcades.

Sidebone — Ossification (changing to bone) of the lateral cartilages of the coffin bone.

Sinusitis — Inflammation of the sinuses.

Splints — This condition involves primarily the interosseous ligament (suspensory) between the large and small metacarpal (less frequently the metatarsal) bones (splint bones). This reaction is a periostitis with production of new bone.

Stringhalt (springhalt) — An affliction of one or both hind legs manifested by spasmodic over-flexion of the joints during progression.

Tendon — The soft tissue structure that connects muscle to bone.

Tendonitis — Inflammation of the tendon.

Thrush — Infection of the frog area of the foot.

Twitch — A device used to gain restraint and control over the horse.

Uveitis — Inflammation of the eye; also called moonblindness.

Ventricle — Two of the four chambers of the heart.

Wind puff — Distension of the tendon sheath with excessive synovial fluid.

Wolf teeth — The first premolar tooth, which is generally absent in most horses.

INDEX

RECOMMENDED READINGS

Blakely, J. *Horses and horse sense: The practical science of horse husbandry*. Reston, Va.: Reston Publishing Company, Inc., 1981.

Draper, J. *Caring for your horse: The comprehensive guide to successful horse and pony care, stable management, equipment, grooming and first aid*. New York: Smithmark Publishers, 1997.

Evans, J W. *Horses: A guide to selection, care, and enjoyment*. New York: W. H. Freeman and Company, 1989.

Siegal, M. ed. *UC Davis Book of Horses*. New York: HarperCollinsPublishers, Inc., 1996.

Adams, OR. and Stashak, TS. *Lameness in Horses*. 4th Ed. Philadelphia: Lea & Febiger, 1987.

Ball, M A. *Understanding Equine First Aid*. Lexington, Ky: The Blood-Horse, Inc., 1998.

Sellnow, L. *Understanding Equine Lameness*. Lexington, Ky: The Blood-Horse, Inc., 1998.

Redden, R. *Understanding Laminitis*. Lexington, Ky: The Blood-Horse, Inc., 1998.

Briggs, K. *Understanding Equine Nutrition*. Lexington, Ky: The Blood-Horse, Inc., 1998.

Jurga, F. *Understanding The Equine Foot*. Lexington, Ky: The Blood-Horse, Inc., 1998.

Picture Credits

CHAPTER 1
Anne M. Eberhardt, 11-13.

CHAPTER 2
Michael A. Ball, 16, 18-20; Anne M. Eberhardt, 21, 23;
Barbara D. Livingston, 22.

CHAPTER 3
Anne M. Eberhardt, 24-25, 27-28; Tim Brockhoff, 26.

CHAPTER 4
Anne M. Eberhardt, 30, 32-33.

CHAPTER 5
Anne M. Eberhardt, 34, 36, 39, 37.

CHAPTER 6
Cheryl Manista, 49.

CHAPTER 7
Tom Hall, 54; Anne M. Eberhardt, 56, 58, 63, 65-68, 72, 74- 75;
Michael A. Ball, 69-71.

CHAPTER 8
Anne M. Eberhardt, 82-83, Ric Redden; 84.

CHAPTER 9
Anne M. Eberhardt, 91, 101; Benoit & Associates, 95; Michael A. Ball, 110.

CHAPTER 10
Michael A. Ball, 115; Anne M. Eberhardt, 115-116.

CHAPTER 11
Anne M. Eberhardt, 121; Kendra Bond, 123.

CHAPTER 12
Anne M. Eberhardt, 128, 130; Michael A. Ball, 132.

EDITOR — JACQUELINE DUKE
COVER/BOOK DESIGN — SUZANNE C. DEPP
ILLUSTRATIONS — ROBIN PETERSON
COVER PHOTO — ANNE M. EBERHARDT

About the Author

Michael A. Ball, DVM, a native of upstate New York, worked professionally in the horse industry for six years before earning a bachelor's degree in animal science from the College of Agriculture and Life Sciences at Cornell

Michael A. Ball, DVM

University and subsequently a degree in veterinary medicine, also from Cornell. After Cornell, he completed an internship in large animal medicine and surgery and also served as an instructor in the Department of Anesthesia at the University of Georgia.

After Georgia, Ball returned to Cornell and completed a residency in large animal internal medicine and the requirements for a Master of Science degree in pharmacology.

Currently holding a faculty position in the Department of Pharmacology, he is board eligible with the American College of Veterinary Internal Medicine and the College of Veterinary Clinical Pharmacology. In addition to his academic pursuits in internal medicine and clinical pharmacology, Ball maintains a strong interest in clinical practice related to performance horses of all types and devotes a substantial effort to owner education on equine health issues. He is the author of *Understanding Equine First Aid*, part of The Horse Health Care Library series, and a frequent contributor to *The Horse* magazine. He lives in Ithaca, N.Y., with his wife, Christina Cable, also a veterinarian.